I'll NEVER be
a HAND MODEL

(and other stories i tell my therapist)

By
Sarah Lemire

woodhall press
Norwalk, CT

Library of Congress Cataloging-in Publication Data available

ISBN Paperback 978-1-949116-41-0

First edition

Cover design by: Libby Kingsbury
Formatting: Libby Kingsbury

Woodhall Press, 81 Old Saugatuck Road, Norwalk, CT 06855
woodhallpress.com

Distributed by IPG

For Michael, Elizabeth & Jayne,
the planets around which I orbit

And, Julia Roberts,
who I'm pretty sure will play me in the movie version

Foreword

Let's be honest, forwards are super-boring and you'll probably skip right over this to get to the questionably "good" stuff.

However, there's a 20% off T.J. Maxx coupon at the end, which you can clip out and use the next time you're shopping for sensible sneakers, potentially making the following paragraphs worth your while.

In 2008, while waiting at a Starbucks to meet a friend who was, as usual, running late, I picked up a copy of *Hartford Magazine* and began paging through it. Prior to that moment, I didn't even know it existed and certainly had no idea that my dire need for a decaf, venti latte with sugar-free vanilla syrup would end up being life-changing.

Having just turned 40, and stayed home with kids for 14 years, I was in the midst of an existential crisis, contemplating everything from returning to my career in television news to going back to college for a master's degree.

Instead, I went home and looked up the magazine's website, where I saw the bold, "Interns Wanted," post and with no hesitation, I applied.

Not long after, Lynn Woike, the editor, called and when I explained that I wasn't a fresh-faced journalism student looking for school credit, but a middle-aged mom seeking a new chapter, she laughed and said, "Why not?"

So, after thanking The Academy and Foreign Press, it's Lynn I begin with. Without her, I'd still be baking cupcakes for playgroup.

My only goal as an unpaid intern was to have a single article published and gave myself a year to accomplish it. Carol Latter made it happen in less than two months. Twelve years later, she continues to be one of the most talented, generous, supportive editors (and friend) anyone could ask for.

When the *Hartford Courant* took over the magazine, I reached out to its new editor, Naedine Hazell, who loved a humorous story I penned about my experience of embarking on a diet detox. Enterprising as always, I told her that there was plenty more where that came from, and because she agreed to let me keep writing, as did Nancy Schoeffler, this book exists.

Before the music swells and we cut to commercial, I have a few more names to drop like Sallie Randolph and Gwen Kesten (you both know why), Nathaniel and Woodhall Press, the most patient people, like, *ever*, and the *Hartford Courant* for giving me the back page of the magazine and a tiny picture to go with it.

I also want to give a shout-out to the kids who wouldn't push over to let me sit down on Bus 28 and that picked me last for their dodgeball team, the friends and family who still talk to me despite knowing my deal, and Sue, who I occasionally beat in Words With Friends and who told me it was OK to quit my job.

Most of all, thanks to my mom, dad, and brother, David, along with my husband, Mike, and daughters, Elizabeth and Jayne, for giving me permission to expose and ridicule them on a regular basis.

Finally, as you may have noticed, there isn't a T.J. Maxx coupon. I lied about that part. But, also, as everyone knows, they don't exist. So that one's on you.

The Drop By, Run In, and the Real Me

I OFTEN WONDER WHAT THOSE STICK-FIGURE CAR DECALS WOULD look like if they were more true-to-life.

For instance, if they represented the occupants in my car, one would be just feet sticking out of blankets and a clock displaying a time well past noon to symbolize my oldest daughter. The other it would be a cell phone with two stick-figure hands gripping it for my youngest.

My husband's would be a confused-looking guy standing in front of the refrigerator, asking where something directly in front of him is.

Mine would be a not-so-stick figure with uncontrollable frizzy hair, wearing flannel pajamas, and dirty slippers, standing amid a towering pile of laundry. Though not very flattering, it'd be pretty accurate, which is why I go to great lengths to hide my true self from the outside world.

In the presence of anyone outside my immediate family, I like to pretend that the "Real Me" dresses like an extra on the set of Project Runway and lives in a home organized by the Container Store.

In reality, however, I live one step up from a barnyard animal.

On any given day, things are growing mold on my laundry room floor, items in my refrigerator are subject to a careful smell-inspection before consumption, and I'm usually wearing some portion (if not all) of what I slept in.

The rest of my family isn't much better. Without any place to be, my teens have gone entire weekends without brushing their teeth or leaving their rooms. On occasion my husband can be found wearing something from what I like to call the, "Day Wear/Night Wear/Day Wear" collection, consisting of the same t-shirt and shorts worn for more than thirty-six hours.

Once, after weeks of living in third world conditions, my

daughter finally cleaned her room and discovered a dead mouse still stuck in the trap on the floor of her closet. It had been left as an offering by our cat, evidently too lazy to do the job himself.

I suppose this is why the unexpected Drop-By is extremely anxiety-provoking.

Even when the UPS guy rings the doorbell, I break out in a cold sweat fearing it might be a friend or neighbor stopping by, forcing me to make unplanned small talk in my bathrobe. Or worse yet, have to invite them in so they can tour my lint ball exhibition.

A few years ago, I set up a meeting at my house with one of my daughter's preschool committee members. Par for the course, I forgot. That is until the doorbell rang midafternoon and wearing cat-hair covered clothes, a prolific amount of zit cream on my face, and every toy we'd ever purchased littering the floor of the living room, I had no choice but to let him in.

Coming in second to the Drop-By is the similarly themed Run-In. This only occurs when I take the calculated risk of doing one *quick* errand wearing something from the latest Day Wear/ Night Wear/ Day Wear collection and incorrectly assuming that I won't see anyone I know.

My favorite episode of the Run-In happened after making a last-minute dash to the post office at closing time without any sort of preliminary grooming. After inspecting the parking lot for recognizable cars and deeming it safe, I darted in only to find myself in line behind the one friend who is the living version of a J. Crew catalog.

It wasn't bad enough that I was wearing a stained t-shirt with one of my daughter's discarded Scrunchies stuck in my hair, but I had recently held a garage sale and was holding a ripped Ziploc bag full of quarters I was looking to get rid of.

Like a peasant from a Dickens novel, I fished quarters out, one by one, and paid for my package, all while making agonizing small talk about Disney World time shares.

Though I tried explaining that I had just come from cleaning my house (an acceptable lie) and the garage-sale quarters, she just smiled knowingly at me and I stopped talking.

Maybe someday I'll actually get it together and live the fictionalized version of my life that I regularly attempt to pass off as real. And then again, as long as those stick figure car decals continue to just represent cheerleaders, soccer moms, and other normal looking people, the only thing I have to worry about is the doorbell.

One Flu Over the Cuckoo's Nest

IT HAPPENS AT LEAST ONCE A YEAR. I CAN ALMOST ALWAYS TELL it's coming by the anxious, questioning look on his face when he says, "Hon…?"

I wait for it.

"Why am I sick?"

After more than three decades together, I'm still not sure if my husband actually wants me to answer this with some sort of comprehensive explanation of white blood cells, microorganisms, the causal correlation they have with viral infections and their substantial influence on human biology. Or if it's simply a rhetorical question meant to inspire me to call 9-1-1, or at the very least tuck the blankets up under his chin and assure him in a soothing voice that he'll live another day to take the garbage out.

As for me, I never question why I'm sick.

Instead I need to know how I got sick and, more important, *who* got me sick so that I can channel my scorching blame onto the individual responsible for the spontaneous expulsion of every fluid in my body, including some that I didn't even know I was capable of producing.

Using fingerprint powder and an evidence collection kit, I'm compelled to retrace every step leading up to the first sniffle in hopes of identifying the unseen benefactor who coughed all over the grocery store credit card machine prior to check out, leaving behind a germ inheritance for me to collect.

Even worse is if the donor is someone I know. Someone who willfully stopped by my house, met me for lunch, or came home from school knowing that they were harboring some form of Dengue Fever, yet neglected to mention it.

This happened one year when a family member showed up to Christmas dinner with their son who'd been throwing up the five preceding days and then used the old "It-Was-Probably-Something-He-Ate" excuse.

Let's take a quick break for a pathology lesson right now.

While I'm no doctor, I'm pretty sure that unless your kid has eaten a casserole of raw hamburger and uncooked eggs, they probably aren't going to vomit for seventy-two hours from anything other than a stomach virus so highly contagious that everyone located within a city mile should avoid eating tacos for the foreseeable future.

And, in this instance, they shouldn't be allowed to leave the house unless they are in a decontamination tent being transported to the nearest quarantine base camp, let alone go out in public or attend family gatherings.

Anyway, shortly after Contagion Christmas, me, my husband, and both kids were simultaneously awarded an extended holiday with our household collection of plastic buckets.

We dined on clear fluids and saltines. When sitting upright was possible, we watched cartoons on the Disney Channel until one scene showed Winnie the Pooh swirling round, round, and around some more, holding a jar of honey and I had to run for the bathroom.

For nearly a week our house resembled a trauma center.

People were randomly lying on the floor. There was excessive moaning, crying and pleas for it to end that only subsided when my husband napped.

Going forward, that incident marked a new chapter in my life, one I like to call the "Hand Sanitizer Years."

No outing of any kind was permitted without a two-liter bottle of Purell in tow and infection checkpoints were established at all family gatherings. If anyone was dripping, coughing, wheezing, sniffing or burping, they were turned away at the door.

Even so, there were still some occasional security breaches. Once, I caught a head cold so bad that I filled a kitchen-sized Hefty bag with crumpled, wet tissues in under two hours, which

I'm pretty sure qualifies as some kind of record. Not even toilet paper stuffed into my nostrils like makeshift sandbags and a tourniquet fastened around my neck could stop the surge.

I got over it, of course. But not before first passing it on to my husband.

"Hon…?"

Fantasy Football

Somewhere between middle and high school, right around the time my hormones were reporting more traffic than the Port Authority, I started watching football.

It wasn't because I was into sports. In fact, far from it. What caught my attention was the appealing buffet of butts in an assortment of shapes and sizes; all poured into fitted, white football pants.

Butts, butts, and more butts. That's the only reason I watched football. On Monday nights, occasional Saturday afternoons and most Sundays, I presided as the official Mayor of Buttropolis, Governor of Gluteustown, and Chairman of the Behind.

Not so different from an episode of "Baywatch," the plot was totally irreverent, the storyline ancillary, and it didn't matter who was in it. As long as there were slow motion replays and linebackers, I was parked in front of the television.

After years of duly serving as a Spectator of the Seat, I eventually transitioned from watching a bunch of guys bending over and doing complicated maneuvers with balls, to actually watching the games and became a fan.

Though I'm no John Madden (even if I do vaguely resemble him after a day or two without a shower), I know enough about the game to be dangerous, and have been known to try to talk football with other fans who, more often than not, fall into the testosterone-filled category. It never goes well.

At family gatherings my husband's dad and brother-in-law usually talk right over me if I bring up draft picks or two-point conversions. Occasionally, if they do listen, it's with wide eyes and puzzled expressions as if I'd suddenly started speaking in binary code.

I'm never sure if it's because 1) I'm a former Minnesota

Vikings fan, which, OK, I understand, or, 2) I'm a girl and sometimes want to talk about Tom Brady's passing game and purchasing new throw pillows in the same conversation.

Whatever the reason, they still permit me into the sacred football TV room during games, which is a lot like a maximum-security prison during lunchtime. It's chaotic, loud and it's possible that someone could get shanked reaching for the buffalo chicken dip.

I'm actually surprised that they let me in at all and not just because I have estrogen. Throughout the years I've come to realize that there are only two kinds of football fans; normal people and rabid, saliva-spitting screamers who suffer some sort of complete emotional breakdown in the minutes between timeouts and commercial breaks.

For the sake of full disclosure, I'm the latter.

I'm not sure why, but the minute I see a play clock, I go from peacefully clipping BJ's coupons to battling the urge to smear on face paint and smash a beer can into my forehead.

That probably explains why the non-football members of our family make a hasty retreat to a separate TV room where they can watch stuff like Giada De Laurentiis making pasta dishes from stick butter and bacon while still not weighing more than a postage stamp.

Once, after I nearly blacked out from a fit of rage during a football game, my mother-in-law ventured from the Food Network room with the same look she has when she gets something she didn't want for Christmas.

"The sound of your voice," she said accentuating each syllable, "feels like someone driving nails into my head."

I can't blame her. I'm sure it's like listening to a civil defense siren going off for the better part of three hours with only halftime and wine refills to break it up.

This was no more apparent than during a recent Super Bowl. At the moment the Patriots intercepted the Seahawks to win the game I shrilled uncontrollably like a tea kettle left on the stove at full boil, then promptly wet my pants a little.

It counts as the single best day of my life right after fitting back into pre-maternity clothes and eating my first Dairy Queen Blizzard.

I admit, however, that despite my unflinching fandom, I still don't know everything about football. In fact, I have no idea what a tight end is or even does.

But I can tell you this much: I know one when I see it.

The Rise and Fall of the Western Omelet

I'm not much into making resolutions. That's probably because, statistically, the likelihood of me sticking to any of them falls somewhere between an imminent alien invasion and the shoes I like going on sale at Zappos.

But that doesn't stop me from trying.

There comes a day each January, sometime after New Year's, but before the Super Bowl, that I realize it's no longer acceptable to continue my daily ritual of eating a dozen or so Christmas cookies and anything covered in gravy, under the "Eat-Whatever-You-Want-Because-It's-The-Holidays" clause.

Around that same time, the bills from my excessive holiday shopping, which sometimes includes gifts for other people, roll in, proving once and for all that money doesn't grow on trees or in my bank account.

It's then that I swear off Marshalls and chocolate-covered Oreos in a concerted effort to get it all back into some semblance of control.

For the first few days I'm unflappable in my commitment.

Determined to transform myself into a pillar of self-discipline and responsibility, I read Suze Orman articles and make grocery lists for my new and improved diet plan, consisting mostly of carrot sticks, brown rice, and yogurt.

On average, I make it less than a week.

Typically, it's a Target clearance rack or the desire to eat something that doesn't taste like a paper towel that's responsible for my downfall, and months pass before I work up enough motivation to try again.

Last year, I resolved to "get serious" about my health and save the world at the same time by becoming a vegetarian.

In the '90s, I also became a vegetarian. It was around the same time that I decided to cut off all my hair, dye it red, and seriously contemplated tattooing a large, blue and green image of the earth on my ankle.

Thankfully, some measure of common sense prevailed, and I decided to hold off until I was certain of what I wanted to permanently emblazon on my body, till death do us part.

A decade later, I went for it anyway. Instead of a planet inked on my ankle, I'm now the proud owner of a generic butterfly on my back.

Regardless, during that first pass at vegetarianism, I was devout. I consumed veggie burgers and tofu while turning down meatballs, Thanksgiving turkey, barbeque ribs and all things worth living for.

After two years, it abruptly ended when, passing by a McDonald's, I turned around and ordered the two-cheeseburger meal at the drive-thru window, effectively concluding The Meatless Period with little to no fanfare.

My most recent attempt was even less successful.

Lasting merely five weeks, it began shortly after I decided that the world and my waistline would be better off if I simply stopped eating meat.

This proved to be false.

Apparently, swapping out protein for vast quantities of pasta, rice, and bread can result in an almost instant upgrade in pants size, along with the need to binge-watch "Daredevil" on Netflix.

Even more, the world hardly seemed to take notice of my considerable sacrifice.

Still, I remained steadfast despite attending any number of social events where I was forced to eat only side dishes while explaining why I had to pass on the medium-rare ribeye.

In the end, it was not steak or Five Guys, but an omelet that did me in.

Out to breakfast with my family, the aroma of bacon, sausage and eggs all mixed up with pancakes and syrup assailed my senses and I felt my resolve begin to weaken. Scanning the menu, I searched for options that would provide a satisfying, meat-free alternative, but my eyes kept darting back to the Western Omelet.

Onions, peppers, cheese and diced ham. Onions, peppers, cheese and diced ham.

And just like that, it was all over.

Not only did I gobble down my omelet, ham and all, I ate everyone else's meat, too, with a cursory, "You gonna eat that?" before reaching across the table to take it off their plate.

This year, I've decided to skip resolutions altogether since I don't seem to be very good at keeping them. Besides, with Christmas cookies still in the freezer and a McDonald's five minutes from my house, it's unlikely that I'm going to save the world anytime soon.

The Tyra Banks of Hand Models

WHEN I WAS LITTLE, MY MOM ACCIDENTALLY SHUT MY HAND IN the door of our tan, wood-paneled station wagon.

Back in the days of no seat belts or fancy automobile safety features of any kind, I had been hanging out of the car door waiting for her to finish putting groceries in the back, when she came around and pushed it closed.

I don't really remember much of what happened after that other than the emergency room doctor admonishing me for crying too much over what was obviously just a simple thumb amputation.

Nineteen stitches and a roll of gauze later, my mom brought me home. Riddled with guilt, she apologized, but not for having shut my hand in the door. Instead, she said she was sorry for having ruined my chances of ever being a hand model.

And she should have been.

When I look at my stocky fingers, bleeding hangnails, and the crescent-shaped scar on my right thumb, I mourn the loss of what could have been a lucrative career.

If it weren't for my mom's negligence, I could've been somebody. I could've had fame and fortune as the Tyra Banks of hand models, draping pearls across my knuckles or gently rubbing lotion on age spots for magazine ads and commercials. I might have even had my own reality TV show where young hopefuls with tapered fingers and perfect cuticles compete against one another for a contract on "America's Next Top Hand Model."

I try not to hold it against her.

I also try to forgive the fact that of all the local pediatricians in my hometown, my parents settled on a German doctor named Mildred Schaffhausen, It didn't matter if I was there for pink eye or head lice, Dr. Schaffhausen always insisted on ending every appointment with at least one shot, if not more.

Once after receiving penicillin injections in each of my legs for an apparent case of strep throat, I gingerly made my way out into the waiting room. "Don't walk funny," my mom sharply reprimanded. "You'll scare the other children."

In hindsight, I should have pulled the fire alarm and implored them to run for their lives, ear infections, croupy coughs and all.

But, fearing repercussion, I remained silent and did my best to walk as if the doctor hadn't just plunged a couple of knitting needles into my upper thighs and then been ordered by my mom to pretend it never happened.

Of course, that was a long time ago and we can joke about it now. That's probably because after having kids of my own, I've come to realize that my mom didn't corner the market on what not to say or do as a parent.

When my oldest daughter was in sixth grade, I volunteered to serve as a chaperone at one of her school events. Before long, I noticed that a few of the girls were picking on her as girls sometimes do.

After she came to me in tears, I got down on my knees, tucked her hair behind her ears and told my daughter that everything would be all right and then proceeded to say that if the girls continued their bullying, I'd go over and kick their prepubescent asses.

It was meant to be reassuring and maybe make her laugh a little, too.

Sometime later, I noticed that the mean girls had turned their attention to me. Trying to understand why they were whispering and pointing in my direction, I called my daughter over and asked what was going on.

"I told them," she said.

"Told them what?" I asked.

"That you said you're going to kick their asses."

Even though this occurred a few years ago, I'm pretty sure that even back then, a playgroup mom threatening to beat up a bunch of twelve-year-olds wasn't looked upon favorably by school officials or local law enforcement.

I spent the next week in a cold sweat waiting for flashing lights to appear in my rearview mirror, or the fuzz to show up at the front door and haul me off to the slammer wearing capris and sensible sneakers.

Thankfully, however, I managed to avoid serving an extended sentence in the state penitentiary for attempting to cheer up my kid. Then again, maybe it wouldn't have been so bad. I could have used the extra time to work on my manicure.

What the Hack?

Hardly a day goes by without some inane story on the internet offering up hacks on important stuff like how to use ketchup, or "life-changing" ways to style curly hair. There are even hacks for streamlining your time in the bathroom.

I don't get it. Can knowing how to style curly hair really change lives? Do we need to figure out how to make peeing more time-effective? And just how many ways are there to use ketchup anyway?

According to the spate of stories on the Internet, even our genders are in need of hacks. One article laments that, gosh, "Being a girl can be challenging from time to time," and because of that, hacks are a "must" for survival. It goes on to provide suggestions on how to break in new flats with a hair dryer, de-fuzz a sweater using a pumice stone and make your own bulletin board from used wine corks.

Considering that during any given week I could fill a dumpster with used wine corks, the last one might prove useful. Otherwise, as a girl, I'm pretty sure that among the difficult challenges in my life, few have required insider knowledge on how to remove little balls from my sweater.

Lazy girls, apparently, need a lot of hacks. There are lazy girl makeup hacks, beauty hacks, fitness hacks and cleaning hacks. There are also a lot of lazy girl hairstyle hacks including the best ways to deal with dirty hair. One recommends that lazy girls simply "Use dry shampoo before bed; it works better and will suck up all the excess oil."

Certainly, that *is* a good tip in lieu of the more difficult challenge of maintaining basic hygiene through bathing of some kind.

Along with lazy girls, there are hacks for "On-the-Go

Modern Gals," because if you aren't a lazy girl, you're obviously super busy and require your very own set of shortcuts.

Moms also need hacks because, as one article puts it, "Being a mom means lots of things, including having savvy knowledge about certain things that your friends who aren't moms probably don't have."

Wait, what?

There are also "Mom Hacks for Real Moms." I like that one, because why should fake moms be privy to any of the secret real-mom tricks?

Women and "gals" aren't the only ones who need hacks. They have them for guys, too.

One story doles out "Essential Manly Life Hacks," offering helpful suggestions on everything from lasting longer in bed (think about baseball), to drinking beer in the shower (it will supposedly change your life), or how to make your own beef jerky (don't ask), and even on how to avoid backsplash in the urinal.

While I'm not a guy, I'd like to think that peeing in a urinal is something that hardly requires a set of guidelines, and if it does, then you've got bigger problems than avoiding backsplash.

Even pet owners have their own hacks like "Puuuurrrfect Hacks Every Cat Owner Should Know," and "Crazy Genius Life Hacks for Dog Owners."

There are also hacks for sleepless cat owners, new dog owners; hacks on how owners can save their puppies' lives, how pet owners can save time, and also for pet owners who are simply too busy to take care of their dog or cat.

I can't help but wonder that if you're looking up hacks on how to carve out time to care for your pet, then perhaps you should reconsider owning one.

But the hacks don't stop there. Every day there are hacks for travel, cooking, working, decorating, driving and just about everything else we do on a regular basis.

I'm not sure why we need so many of them and frankly, I'm

tired of reading snappy suggestions and so-called hacks like the one I saw recently on how to order teas at Starbucks "that are more refreshing than Frappes!"

It bothers me so much that I complained about it to my teenage daughter, griping about how everyone seems obsessed with finding shortcuts for everything under the sun.

"You're weird," she said, and then proceeded to shut me down in one sentence. "If you're so against shortcuts, then maybe you should stop using the dryer."

Enough said.

Happy Brother's Day

JOHN DENVER WAS THE LOVE OF MY LIFE. WITH HIS ROUND glasses, shaggy blond hair, and wholesome songs about nature, he embodied everything a seven-year-old girl could ever want from a man who'd one day sing with the Muppets.

Countless hours of my young life were spent yodeling along with John about mountain mammas in West Virginia and thanking God he was a country boy.

That is, of course, until my brother ruined it.

With nothing better to do one summer day, David, five years my senior, found me in the backyard as I played with Ken and Malibu in their swanky plastic house with the pull string elevator.

"You know," he said, "John Denver changed his name when he got famous. That's not his real name."

Convinced that he was lying, I vehemently argued that "John Denver" was indeed John Denver, future husband to me, Mrs. Sarah Denver. The man I would one day marry and together we'd enjoy a lifetime of sunshine on our shoulders.

"No, his real name is Henry Deutschendorf," he corrected. "So, if you get married, you'll be Sarah Deutschendorf."

Sarah Deutschendorf?

Over my shrieking protests, he repeated the name again and again until, on the verge on a complete breakdown, he delivered the final blow.

"Oh yeah, he smokes pot, too. What do you think 'Rocky Mountain High' is about?"

I lay on my back in the grass and cried as Dave walked away, satisfied with completing yet another successful mission and already making plans for the next one.

And there was always a next one.

Once, my brother spent an entire morning carefully folding pieces of notebook paper into perfect little munitions. After he'd accumulated a considerable arsenal in his school pencil box, he spent the rest of the day deftly firing them all at me from a giant rubber band stretched across his fingers as I ran screaming through the house.

Though well-executed, it wasn't his best work. The pièce de résistance came with his inspired use of the Kodak Instamatic.

As a kid I suffered from a nearly incapacitating fear of lightning.

With the proficiency of a meteorologist, I'd watch developing weather like it was my job. If there were dark skies, watches, warnings or mild fluctuations in barometric pressure, I'd be holed up in the basement praying for survival from the impending apocalypse.

So great was my anxiety that even a camera flash was enough to send me into a full, sweaty panic. Subsequently, every indoor photograph taken in my early childhood is of me looking down or my face pressed into someone's arm.

Using my disability to his advantage, Dave liked to spend his free time calling me into his room under the pretense of having something he wanted to show me. He'd quietly wait on the other side of the door with his camera and when I walked in, FLASH!

Dissolving immediately into tears, I'd lock myself in my room for the rest of the day. Eventually after enough time elapsed, I'd forget. When I was least expecting it, he'd call out my name and naively I'd go to find out what he wanted. FLASH!

I give him credit, he never tired of the game and because of it, there's an entire collection of photographs of me standing in his doorway wearing an expression of shocked bewilderment in all of them.

Finally, I caught on and refused to oblige when he'd call. But he was relentless in his pursuit.

One afternoon he called my name over and over. "Please," he said, "I swear to God, I promise I won't use the flash. I just want to show you something. I swear on my life. *Swear to God.* I. Swear. To. God."

If he was swearing to God and on his own life, then I had no choice but to believe him. So, I went. FLASH!

I wonder if condemning his soul to hell for all of eternity was worth getting me one last time. I'm guessing if I asked him, he'd probably say it was.

When Mother's Day rolls around, I'll probably get my mom some flowers and invite her over for lunch to thank her for everything she's done for me.

I'm thinking of doing the same for my brother. However, instead of roses, I've been busy folding notebook paper and recently purchased a pencil box. I also plan on charging my camera battery because there's something in my room that I want to show him.

Shoppers Anonymous

I OFTEN WONDER IF SHOPPING ADDICTION MEETINGS BEGIN WITH a modified form of the Serenity Prayer.

> *God grant me the serenity to accept my credit limit. The courage to pass up that All-Clad saucepan. And the wisdom to know the difference between shoes that seem comfortable when I try them on, but cause blisters once it's too late to return them.*

Though I've never actually been to one, I'm pretty sure I qualify.

In fact, I'm convinced that one day I'm going to come home (weighted down with department store bags in each hand) and discover concerned family members, friends, and TJ Maxx cashiers gathered in my living room holding bank statements and store receipts, prepared to have an "honest conversation."

I confess. It would be warranted.

Given the choice between doing yoga and shopping to find my own private Idaho, I routinely pick the latter. In my defense, however, I could argue that they really aren't all that different.

Instead of doing the Downward-Facing Dog, I do the Downward-Facing Dig, a pose which occurs when I'm frantically flipping through a pile of smartly folded sale sweaters at the Gap hoping there's still one medium left.

When confronted by another shopper who's going in for the same clearance item that I am, I like to break out the Cobra to indicate my readiness to strike if necessary.

And if I'm armed with gift cards or have paid off my most recent credit card bill, I'm channeling the Warrior, because with money to burn, I'm most likely planning to shop like one.

Much like yoga, when I'm finished with my session, I almost

always feel relaxed, peaceful and mildly sweaty from exertion.

Perhaps that's why I like the holidays so much. It's the time of year when shopping becomes mandatory and I don't have to work so hard to find an excuse. It's like court-appointed community service, I'm required to do it.

With a gift list in hand and a half-smile on my face, I wander the aisles listening to K.D. Lang sing about a constant craving from overhead speakers (subliminal messaging no doubt), and dreamily put sweaters, scarves, pajamas, wine glasses, jewelry, and, occasionally, stuff for other people in my cart.

Unfortunately, it almost always ends too soon and inevitably along the way to the checkout counter I'm forced to do what I like to call the Grenade Maneuver.

This emergency tactic becomes essential once I realize than I have more items in my cart than money and have four seconds to ditch anything I don't want to explode on my next Visa bill before reaching the cashier.

Once I get home and unpack my bounty, I almost immediately regret at least one purchase.

Typically, it's something like a twenty-four pack of Santa Claus martini glasses I grabbed in case I actually have the holiday cocktail party I've been planning since *Seinfeld* was still on primetime.

More often than not, however, it's some fashion-don't for women over forty like skinny jeans, which in my case are called "I-Wish-I-Were" jeans.

These items are then bagged up and deposited into the back of my car where they ride around for weeks before I bring myself to do the only thing I don't like about shopping – returns.

I'm not sure how it works exactly, but I'm convinced that some law of physics governs that no matter how carefully I've packaged up my return, an item I have never worn, tried on, or even looked at after leaving the store, upon being pulled from the bag by a clerk, will appear as though I used it as a lint roller at an animal shelter or at the very least, wore it to hike the entire Appalachian Trail before deciding I didn't want it.

Moreover, once the rovers that have been dispatched to explore black holes in outer space begin transmitting images back to earth, I'm fairly certain they'll show pictures of all the receipts that I've judiciously tucked into my wallet in case I need to return something, only to find them missing every time I do.

But I guess that's alright, because without a receipt I can usually still get store credit. And there's only one thing I can really do with it.

Shop.

TMI

By nature, I'm a curious person and like to know things. For instance, I'd like to know why a single cigarette ash can burn down an entire national park, but using a box of Duraflame starters, the Sunday paper, and a squirt of lawnmower gas, I still can't manage to ignite a fire in my own fireplace.

I'd also want to know why, no matter what strategy I employ, I always pick the grocery line where someone needs a price check on kelp powder or is using a coupon that requires a manager intervention and global summit over a thirty-five-cent discount on Frank's Hot Sauce.

After hours of frustrating negotiations, I sometimes just want to fish a twenty out of my purse and offer to buy everyone out if we can agree to drop the whole thing.

There's also a lot of stuff I don't want to know but somehow manage to stumble across while looking up cat videos on the internet. Most of the time it involves celebrities and the creepy things they reveal.

Back when Kim and Kayne tied the knot it was widely reported that they choose to have the wedding in Italy because it's where they conceived their baby. While that's charming and everything, I'm not sure why I need to know this and wonder at what age their child will find out the big secret behind mom and dad's favorite vacation spot.

I'm pretty sure that if my kids ever found out where they were conceived, they'd spend the rest of their lives attempting to erase it from their collective memory, let alone plan some kind of vacation there. But since they've already been upstairs, I probably don't have to worry about it.

Not long ago, I came across an article about Martha Stewart who apparently confessed to sexting on her phone and admitted that she "might" have had a threesome.

I've always admired Martha and her ability to crochet turkey platters from old bed sheets. Although this new, and uncomfortable, information hasn't lessened my appreciation for her considerable talents, it has provided me with a fresh perspective whenever I hear her say "It's a good thing."

Thanks to a celebrity gossip website, I recently learned that after the birth of her first child, former Playboy model Holly Madison had her placenta turned into vitamin pills that she could take to assist in her recovery.

Despite all the health benefits that I'm sure are associated with it, there are mornings I find it difficult to get a poached egg down let alone ingest something that passed through an orifice of my body; regardless of what form someone has managed to fashion it into.

I also read once that when her son was an infant, actress Alicia Silverstone chewed up his food before spitting it into his mouth for him to eat.

For the sake of transparency, I confess that for a brief period of time while I was in elementary school, I picked up the habit of chewing ABC gum for no other reason than it was there, and I could. Which still doesn't make it right.

Anyway, in addition to the food thing, Silverstone also named her son Baby Bear Blu.

I admit it has a certain ring to it and that there's a fairly good chance no one else will accidentally raise their hand at the same time during attendance.

Even so, I can't help but wonder if at some point in Baby Bear's life, like during wedding vows or being awarded the Nobel Peace Prize that it might feel a little awkward to be named after a Fisher Price toy.

He's not alone, however, celebrities ranging from Beyoncé to Michael Jackson have given their children weird monikers too.

I sometimes wish we had been more creative in naming our kids. At the time we thought it was pretty controversial adding a completely unnecessary "Y" to the middle of our youngest daughter's first name.

I realize now that with some ingenuity we could have given our girls more impressive names like Bubble Bath McFarty or Solar Panel. If we'd gone the route of Gwyneth Paltrow, who named her daughter Apple after her favorite food, we could have been ordering birthday cakes for Ben & Jerry Alfredo.

Thankfully we decided kept it simple and I'm sure our girls, K8 and Cayenne, are glad we did.

That Seventies Kid

LIKE MOST PEOPLE, JANUARY IS USUALLY WHEN I MAKE A FEW New Year's resolutions.

Typically, they include things like finding a hobby outside of Marshall's Home Goods, swearing off miniature Butterfingers, and replacing the blade on my Pedegg.

But, mostly, when a new calendar year begins, I like to take a moment to remind myself just how fortunate I am.

Oh sure, I'm lucky for all the usual reasons; the air I breathe, a roof over my head, the variety of restaurants that offer pasta dishes.

But more than that, as a child of the seventies, I'm just grateful I made it to adulthood.

Unlike my own kids, who were bubble-wrapped until they turned twenty, I grew up in world where, instead of child-proof caps, Mr. Yuck stickers were the only thing preventing a toddler from snacking on a bottle of baby aspirin and "safety feature" meant your bike seat was padded.

Otherwise, in true Darwin fashion, you were pretty much on your own.

We didn't have stuff like baby monitors and plug covers. In fact, as a kid, my first lesson on electricity came after sticking a hairpin into an outlet and discovering that, not-surprisingly, 120 volts surging through your body feels an awful lot like being set on fire.

The upside is that I learned at a relatively young age exactly what kinds of items should - and should not - be inserted into a wall socket with no further explanation ever needed.

Before our first daughter was born, my husband and I attended an hour-long class on how to use an infant car seat, then practiced in our driveway for another month before bringing her home from the hospital.

Far from being mandatory when I was little, car seats were virtually nonexistent.

Speeding down the freeway in our Ford LTD station wagon, I'd often crawl around from the front seat to the back, while my mom puffed away on a Lark cigarette and listened to Tom Jones cheerily sing about stabbing his cheating girlfriend, Delilah, to death. A tune I'm pretty sure wouldn't share the same mass market appeal if released today.

There was a tailgate on the back of our wagon with a single, enormous window. For fun, my parents would roll the window down and allow my brother and I to sit on top of it as they drove.

It was totally safe, of course, especially considering that we had the roof rack to hold on to.

And since letting go meant tumbling backward onto the road and facing certain death, it provided extra incentive to get a good grip.

These days a stunt like that would practically guarantee some kind of parental jail time, maybe even foster placement. But back then, it was acceptable, if not expected, since, in the absence of Netflix, there was nothing else to do.

Along with an apparent lack of basic common sense, there were also no smartphones to help track your kid's every move.

Thanks to the advent of the text message, I'm available around the clock to respond to any and all my kids' emergencies including, but not limited to, the removal of hangnails, wardrobe consults, selfie therapy, and delivering explicit instructions on how to talk on a telephone.

When I was growing up, my parents had no clue where I was a majority of the time, and as long as I wasn't loitering in the kitchen eating the last of the Twinkies, it didn't matter.

There's a reason the term "helicopter parent" didn't exist in the '70s. There weren't any.

In fact, most days my parents seemed mildly disappointed when I came home from school, as if they'd been hoping that I'd slipped off to college or moved out while they weren't paying attention.

Back then, we also didn't sweat the little things like seatbelts, pesticides, food contamination, asbestos, or second-hand smoke.

No one ate organic or gluten-free. Bike helmets were unheard of, let alone knee and elbow pads, all of which would have come in handy the dozen-or-so times I ate gravel after losing control of my purple Schwinn.

But sometimes I wonder if those really were the good old days? Days when we lived for the moment without technology and child welfare laws to interfere? Days filled with carefree wonder, joy and near-death experiences?

Then I think, nope, and check my phone to see if I have any new text messages.

Good Boy

RECENTLY I RECEIVED A NOTIFICATION THAT MY CELL PHONE storage was full and if I hoped to avoid some kind of nuclear catastrophe where I couldn't play Solitaire or check the forecast on The Weather Channel app, I needed to delete some pictures.

Dutifully obliging, I began sorting through 3,000 saved images only to discover that aside from the photos I'd taken of my husband, kids, friends, vacations, and wine menus, there were 2,992 pictures of my cat.

Like the Picasso of feline photography, I'd chronicled every one of his nine lives through the tiny lens of my iPhone 6.

Buddy reclining. Buddy sitting up. Buddy swatting his roller-ball. Buddy looking out the window. Buddy in repose. Buddy sleeping, stretching, yawning, cleaning, eating, walking, playing, infinitude.

And that's just this past year.

Safely stored on my computer's back-up drive are thousands more, amassed over a decade for display in some future museum exhibit entitled, "Portrait of an Orange Cat: A Retrospective."

In the unlikely event that I missed even a single Buddy moment, I rest easy knowing my daughters and husband have it logged somewhere on their phones, since they're abnormally preoccupied with the cat too.

It's not uncommon for entire conversations to revolve around him, how cute he is, how much we love him, why petting his stomach makes him mad, as well as wondering where he is and what he might be up to.

Rhetorical questions considering that, other than being hunched over his food dish and using the litter box, the only things he's capable of doing are sleeping and shedding all over my clothes, and on any given day, he's somewhere doing both.

We also suffer from an excessive cat accessory problem.

Buddy has a dedicated 'enrichment' drawer in our living room stuffed with crinkly balls, catnip squirrels, fake mice (though based on experience it appears he prefers the real ones) and a laser pointer reserved for special occasions.

He's also the proud owner of an outdoor tent and collection of feline fashionwear.

It's funny, he doesn't seem to enjoy wearing the turtlenecks or Halloween costumes we've picked out for him.

Instead he stands immobilized and unblinking before rigidly falling over, as if wearing a jester's hat or cat sweater is somehow unnatural.

In addition to his given name, we've bestowed a variety of nicknames on him in case he's grown complacent over the years.

Along with "Buddy," he answers to "The Bud Man," "The Budster," "Fluffy," "Orangie," "Cutie Cat," "Fluffernutter," and "Fred Fredburger (don't ask)."

But mostly we just call him, "Good Boy."

A lot.

And for some inexplicable reason, we can't resist asking him if he thinks he's a good boy, too.

As if he'd know the difference.

But that doesn't stop us.

"Where's my good boy?"

"Who's a good boy?

"Is Buddy a good boy?"

I'm not even sure why, since much of the time he isn't.

Even with a prolific number of scratching posts at his disposal, Buddy prefers the Pottery Barn one. Or what we refer to as "the couch."

And for no reason can anyone leave anything perishable on the kitchen counter.

Because while he recognizes that it's strictly verboten when we're around, he takes liberties when we aren't.

Loaves of bread have mysteriously gone missing when left out to thaw, and despite being a large cat, it seems he's able fit his entire head into a drinking glass without much trouble.

He's also developed a taste for gum.

It took several months of chewing moist, sticky pieces of Trident, with no logical explanation of why they were soggy, until eventually walking in on Buddy, busily licking the pack that I like to leave on my desk.

It's hardly surprising since licking seems to be his specialty.

Most days I'm happy that he's got the whole hygiene thing covered without any additional effort on my part.

The rest of the time it's exhausting to watch him wash himself in a contorted pose that a friend once dubbed the "Pretty, Pretty Ballerina."

While I can't vouch for the "pretty" part, I'm convinced that if he practices it for much longer, he'll be invited to go on tour with The Nutcracker.

We wouldn't let him go, of course, we'd miss him too much.

After all, he's a good boy.

The Wager

FOR THE MOST PART, MY HUSBAND AND I AREN'T BIG PRACTICAL jokers.

True, as an April Fool's prank one year, my husband mixed in a generous helping of Bertie Bott's Every Flavor Beans into to a community bowl of Jelly Belly's sitting on his desk at work.

For the uninitiated, Bertie Bott's jellybeans, a candy originating from the *Harry Potter* series, come in a variety of unconventional flavors like earthworm, grass, earwax, laundry detergent, rotten egg, dirt, booger, and vomit.

Having sampled nearly all of them for authenticity, I can confirm they bear a striking resemblance to their real-life counterparts, despite not having actually eaten most of those things. At least not laundry detergent.

Grabbing a handful while coming to discuss some computer networking thing, my husband's boss was the first pioneer to discover what soap, vomit, earwax, and strawberry cheesecake taste like when consumed in a single bite.

Though I wasn't there, I like to listen to my husband recount the moment his boss transitioned from talking routers and IP addresses to expunging everything from his mouth in a violent *ppppfffffttt.* before bewilderingly asking, "What's *IN* these?"

Beyond that, however, neither one of us has ever short-sheeted a bed or sprayed shaving cream into a sleeping, mouth-breather's hand, which I guess is what makes the litter-box cake especially inspired.

It was an ordinary Saturday, when, for no good reason other than guaranteeing future therapy bills, we hatched a scheme to prank our two, elementary-aged daughters.

Having seen a recipe on how to create an edible kitty litter cake, I thought it would be fun to see if I could make one, then convince them that it was real.

First, I went to the grocery store for the ingredients, before hitting up a local pet shop to purchase an exact replica of the litterbox used by our two cats, and a duplicate litter scoop.

Later, in front of our daughters, my husband and I invented a fictitious wager between the two of us, in which the loser would have to eat from the litterbox as the ultimate, absurd consequence.

Far from being appalled at our little bet, they tittered and giggled at the prospect.

The foundation was laid.

Crafting the pièce de résistance took most of the day. The cake had to be baked, crumbled, then mixed with food coloring to get the right shade. Tootsie Rolls were melted in the micro-wave and reshaped to look less like chocolate candy and more like litterbox artifacts.

When all was said and done, the result was a very credible and repulsive reproduction.

To say that I was pleased with myself is an understatement.

That night, as we finished up dinner, my husband brought up the 'wager,' and after a brief discussion, it was agreed that he had lost.

Our daughters howled in delight, gleefully reminding him of his punishment.

At least until the moment I went to the basement, brought up the cake, and set it down in the middle of the kitchen table.

In hindsight, I never expected them to actually buy it. I fig-ured they'd know it was a scam right off the bat, and we'd all have a good laugh while eating cake for dessert.

Instead, a shocked hush fell over the room as they silently contemplated the litterbox, scoop sticking out the side and a single, sculpted Tootsie Roll stuck to the edge for added effect.

One of my daughters looked up at my husband with wide eyes and said, "Daddy, don't."

"I have to, I lost the bet," he replied woefully, before reach-ing in, fishing out a Tootsie Roll, and bringing it to his mouth.

In that instant, complete and total panic erupted as both

girls ran, screaming hysterically, from the room, seeking refuge in an upstairs closet and locking themselves inside.

We went after them, of course.

But it took a while.

Neither of us could manage to get off the floor where we'd fallen, weak and red-faced, eyes streaming, laughing so hard that no sound came out.

Eventually we coaxed them from the closet and now, more than twelve years later, they find it hilarious, telling the story every chance they get.

I, however, am filled with regret. After all, what kind of parents pull a trick like that on their kids?

And then forget to videotape it?

I guess there's always grandchildren.

The Kind You Bring to Parties

I RECENTLY RECONNECTED WITH AN OLD HIGH SCHOOL FRIEND. While catching up over the phone, I asked her to hold on a minute so I could grab my reading glasses.

"Oh," she said. "You wear cheaters?"

This gave me pause. First of all, I'd never really heard that term used outside of infidelity, board games, and my neighbor discussing tax write-offs. Second, I wasn't sure how needing glasses to read anything smaller than a billboard qualified as "cheating."

Most importantly, however, I couldn't help but wonder when I had become my mother.

I'm guessing it happened somewhere around the time when leaving the house after 7:30 p.m. became WAY TOO LATE and I began needing my kids' help to perform some highly technical skill like turning my phone off.

And only just recently have I come to understand that when my daughters talk about "apps" they aren't referring to hotdogs wrapped in crescent dough.

It's like I went to bed one night and woke up the next day to find that, like Rip Van Winkle, I'd been asleep for twenty years and upon staggering to the mirror, discovered that I'd developed more lines on my face than a third grader practicing cursive.

Not surprisingly, it's that same face I see every time I attempt to take a selfie, which on occasion has caused me to audibly gasp after realizing that I'm looking at myself and not Angela Lansbury.

But there's other stuff too. Like when my kids talk about movie actors, it often turns into a game of "Who's on First?" since it's all pretty confusing to me.

"Mom, don't you think Chris Pratt is cute?"

"Isn't he the one engaged to Miley Cyrus?"

"No, mom, you're thinking of Chris Hemsworth. It was his brother, Liam, who was married to Miley Cyrus. They broke up already."

"Then which one is in Star Trek?"

"Mom, that's Chris Pine."

"Wasn't he in The Avengers too?"

"Mom, *no*, that's Chris Evans."

"Isn't he the alien warrior guy sent to earth to fight villains?"

"*That's* Chris Hemsworth, he's cute."

"Wait, I thought you said Chris Pratt was the cute one?"

"He *is* the cute one."

Sigh.

Why do I have to know any of this anyway? I don't have enough free real estate in my brain to keep my own life straight, let alone remember which famous Chris twerked in outer space or whatever.

In fact, without sea of Post-It notes wallpapering my office I don't think I'd remember anything at all.

On a daily basis I write myself notes to remember to send bills, make follow up phone calls, and other essential to-dos.

Unfortunately, the problem I run into is that sometimes when I look at them, I don't actually remember what they mean. There are random dates with no other references, phone numbers with no names, names of people I don't know, passwords for unknown accounts, and even more concerning was the time I found a note scrawled in my handwriting that simply read, "Toilet."

It took a while, but eventually I figured out that I had been trying to remind myself to buy a new toothbrush, but somewhere between leaving the bathroom and finding a piece of paper, the message somehow got lost in translation.

God knows, that could have been a serious mishap right there, as those are two things I don't ever want to cross wires over.

When I was younger, I used to believe that it wouldn't bother me to get older.

Of course, that was long before I realized that one day I would take unrecognizable photos of myself on a phone that I don't know how to turn off and requires the use of the Hubble Telescope if I want to read a text message on it.

If nothing more, at least I know what an app is now. Even if I do still prefer the kind you bring to parties.

Honk If You Use Your Horn

I'm not much of a honker.

In fact, I've owned my car for more than nine years and still have no clue where the horn is.

Typically, when a situation arises requiring its use, I just frantically pound on the steering wheel hoping I might inadvertently hit it.

By the time it finally blares it's usually too late and the need, like clearing running pedestrians from the front of my car, has already passed.

It's not because I don't like the horn, am opposed to the horn, or that I don't understand the value of the horn for things like greeting a familiar passerby, announcing my arrival, or preventing certain death.

I just don't use it.

Instead, if it's necessary to convey my feelings to another driver, I prefer using more universally recognized forms of communication, both verbal and non-verbal, to get my point across.

Some people, however, blow their horn at every opportunity even when there's not a valid reason.

I once had a friend who honked at virtually anything. Real or imagined.

She'd see a car waiting at an intersection. *Beep*. A car preparing to leave a gas station. *Beep*. A car at a stop sign. *Beep*. A car making a legal, left-hand turn. *Beep*.

Finally, when I couldn't stand it any longer, I asked her what she was doing.

"I just want to make sure they know I'm here," she replied.

Based on her overall driving ability, I didn't think it was going to be a problem, but kept that to myself.

A current friend of mine has mastered the remarkable skill

of riding the brakes while simultaneously accelerating in a violation of physics so groundbreaking, even Stephen Hawking couldn't have written a formula for it.

Her "accelerbraking," routinely provokes a significant amount of honking, usually from someone behind her who's unable to tell if she's stopping or attempting time travel.

Though I'm not much of a honker, I've observed that honking has its own set of guidelines and means for interpretation.

The "Would-You-Mind-Looking-Up-From-Your-Phone-Because-The-Light-Has-Been-Green-Since-Last-Week," honk, is a short tap that lets the person in front of you know that while you're doing your very best to be polite, ramming into their vehicle is your next order of business if they don't stop wasting your time checking Instagram.

The longer, bellowing, "Oh-My-God-What-The-Hell-Are-You-Doing," honk is usually reserved for someone who has nearly ended your life with their driving incompetence or is verging on it.

In certain situations it's acceptable to use the more aggressive "What-The-Hell-Are-You-Doing," honk in place of the "Would-You-Mind-Looking-Up-From-Your-Phone," honk, including (but not limited to), when you're speeding to an appointment you forgot you made, just finished a 32-ounce Dunkin' Donuts coffee, or it's Monday.

Occasionally, when the infraction is severe enough, like when a cutter sneaks in line after you've been sitting in traffic waiting to take an exit, you'll hear the "Police-Intervention-Required," honk.

This happens when someone is so unbelievably enraged that they continuously hold down the horn with no intention of releasing it. Ever.

If you're on the receiving end of it, it can only mean one of two things: a driver's ed refresher course is in order, or you're from Massachusetts.

Even if I was a honker, I probably wouldn't use the horn in

my car. It's pretty lame as far as horns go.

It's not like the one in the Ford Country Squire station wagon that we had when I was growing up.

Sounding like a steam engine pulling into the station, our wood-paneled, tank-of-a-car had an impressive horn with a commanding, but pleasant tone saying, "Don't-Even-Consider-Doing-That-Again, But-Have-A-Nice-Day!"

My minivan hardly compares.

On the rare occasion that I've used it, it bleats out a thin, *meeeeeehhhhh*, warning anyone in the vicinity to BACK OFF, because I've got groceries in the car and am headed to a school open house.

Or even more threatening, I'm perimenopausal so they better watch out or else I'll have no choice but to put down my candy bar, cry, then immediately forget anything happened.

Maybe the next car I own will have a horn worth honking. If so, it's possible I might actually use it once in a while. The only downside is that I'll have to find it first.

Dead Plants Society

WHEN IT COMES TO PLANTS, SOME PEOPLE INHERENTLY HAVE A green thumb.

Me? I'm just happy the kids are still around considering my complete inability to grow anything requiring oxygen and water.

It's not from lack of trying. I really like plants and have a decent collection of them scattered throughout the house. Of course, most of them are plastic but even those appear as though they haven't been watered in a while.

The few live ones are of the "hardy" variety, meaning that much like cockroaches, they're able to survive a nuclear winter; the requirement when I bring one home.

It's somewhat surprising since gardening is in my DNA. Growing up, my grandmother loved planting so much that she and my grandfather purchased an acre of land a short distance from their home and turned it into one, big garden they called "The Ponderosa."

As a kid, I loved going to The Ponderosa. There were massive flower beds, rows of lush vegetables, corn stalks, strawberries, raspberries, and a big oak tree with a tire swing that hung from a long branch.

I spent a lot of summer days sitting beneath the shade of that oak. According to my grandmother, one afternoon when I was four, I studied a caterpillar making its way up the side of the tree before asking her where she thought it was going.

She replied that it was probably going home to its family.

I then wondered if the caterpillar had a mother and father, and she said yes.

I asked a couple more philosophical questions before the conversation took an awkward turn.

If my grandmother is to be believed, I also apparently asked if, in name of science and discovery, I could pee on it to see what would happen.

Impossible, really, given the logistics of it all but decidedly uncomfortable, nonetheless.

In her infinite wisdom, she simply asked if I wanted the caterpillar to pee on me, effectively ending the discussion, since I didn't.

Those were some happy memories, which is probably why, despite my botanic limitations, I attempt to put in my own garden every year.

Each spring, like an emperor going into battle, I maneuver my oversized cart, with the single, janky wheel stuck to the left, down the aisles of The Home Depot garden center, looking for soldiers brave enough to join me in the fight.

Though I can't be sure, I'm sometimes get the feeling that some play dead or feign a blight in hopes that I'll keep walking.

I'm no fool, however, I still manage to spot the true warriors, the herbs and vegetables that look hydrated and ready to sacrifice their lives, all in the name of ancestry and horticulture.

Upon arriving home, I unload them from the trunk and judiciously set them near the rocky, clay-packed, dirt patch they'll call home for the summer. Then promptly forget that I ever went to the store.

A week or two later, I remember while checking the mail and by the sheer grace of God and natural selection, a handful survive, so I plant them just for trying.

Feeling guilty, I initially tend to my weakened, fledging annuals like Martha Stewart.

Wearing stylish gardening gloves and pastel pants, I breezily announce to everyone that I'm "going out to the garden," where, for a time, I fastidiously weed and water my plants, all while dreaming of the pesto I'll make with my bumper crop of basil and the salads that will benefit from my garden-fresh cucumbers.

But, as with most things, I eventually run out of steam, complaining that it's just too much work, it's too hot outside, I'm too busy, I need a pedicure, whatever, and neglect settles in.

By mid-August, anything that isn't dead is either crawling with Japanese beetles, or deformed in some spindly way, as though it attempted to grow itself out of the garden and into a place where there might actually be sunlight or water.

It's at around this time that I throw in the towel, swearing off gardening forever, before developing amnesia a year later and do it all over again.

Maybe one day I'll get it right, in honor of my grandmother and The Ponderosa. Then again, there's always Whole Foods, which, last I checked, has plenty of basil and cucumbers, and, as far as I can tell, no caterpillars.

Don't Touch My Hair

I'VE NEVER REALLY HAD NORMAL HAIR. BORN WITH A RARE COMbination of Astro Turf and yarn, it's not straight, not curly, but instead a perpetually damaged-looking hinterland located somewhere in between.

Growing up, I so desperately wanted long, straight hair that in lieu of it I sometimes wore pantyhose on my head. With suntan-colored pigtails sprouting from a control-top panty, I'd run through our yard, stockings trailing behind me, pretending I was one of Charlie's Angels.

For special occasions, I liked to tie or twist them together in a fancy up-do. But for the most part, I just left them down, content to let the nylon tresses fall around my shoulders.

In hindsight, it probably explains why I wasn't asked to hang out after school or invited to many neighborhood birthday parties.

In addition to social suicide, having unmanageable hair meant that my mom was always hauling me off to Betty's, a one-chair beauty salon in the farming community I grew up in.

With a wide Midwestern smile and tortoise shell glasses, Betty wasn't afraid to try out the latest styles pictured in her beauty magazines.

I was the first in town to wear the Dorothy Hamill, which ultimately looked more like the Buster Brown than anything bouncy or Olympic. For most of sixth grade I sported the Orphan Annie, the apparent outcome of doing a perm on someone who already has naturally curly hair.

In high school, a misshapen bobbed haircut left me with curly, Princess Leia side buns.

There were also the Mullet Years. A long stretch of time when I wore Billy Ray Cyrus, achy-breaky-heart-hair after Betty decided to add "a few layers" in order to "lighten it up a little."

Eventually Betty and I broke up and I began seeing a neighbor down the street who liked to cut hair at her kitchen table while sipping on rum and Cokes.

We had a good run, right up until the night Captain Morgan overstayed his welcome and she forgot to shampoo out the chemical solution she'd liberally applied to my scalp.

I spent much of the next year looking like the love child of a Phil Spector, Cyndi Lauper hookup.

I'm pretty sure that I inherited my follicle disability from my mom. Throughout much of my childhood she complained bitterly about her hair, which typically required a full hour of careful preparation before she'd even consider leaving the house.

I can still remember the sound of Aqua Net being emitted in one, long, continuous stream before she'd finally emerge from the bathroom in a cloud of spray.

No one was allowed to get close to her once she was fully shellacked and she'd jerk her head away with an angry "DON'TTOUCHMYHAIR," if we made any sudden movements near her face.

Once, during a long car trip, my brother and I sat in the backseat and passed the time eating a container of strawberries. I don't really know who started it first, but somehow a game of Strawberry Jenga got underway.

Before long, my mom was wearing a crown of half-eaten berries on the back of her head while we each took turns adding more, waiting to see which one would ultimately topple her blonde, backcombed tower.

I don't remember who won but do recall the venomous look in my mother's eyes when she realized we'd been using her beehive for sport.

After years of combating my own disorderly hair, I've settled on the only two styles that I'm able to wear.

The straight version bears more than just a passing resemblance to Quick Curl Barbie, complete with frayed ends and pieces that don't move once you set them in place.

The other option is a tangled mess of frizzy curls that requires working knowledge of the Periodic Table and a hair dryer set to "incinerate" in order to appear as though I tried.

Both require heavy assistance from Paul Mitchell and neither make me look like Selena Gomez.

It usually takes me an hour of careful preparation before I consider leaving the house and sometimes if my husband or kids get too close to my face, I find myself jerking my head back and angrily saying, "DON'TTOUCHMYHAIR." But most days I just try to accept my hair since there's not a whole I can do about it, anyway. And besides, I have a drawer full of pantyhose for when I feel like wearing it long and straight.

Antisocial Media

OF THE EIGHT BILLION HUMAN BEINGS INHABITING PLANET earth, at least one billion of them are on Facebook.

Well, 999,999,999, minus one, anyway.

If you're not interested in performing my complicated algebra, I'll just say it. I'm among the few, the proud, the Facebook-less.

Oh sure, like all the cool kids, I tried it a couple of times. However, I was only pretending and never inhaled. But back to social media, I have to admit, I really just didn't get it.

Right off the bat, I found the whole thing to be a complete time suck. To create my "page," I first had to spend hours sifting through photographs to find ones that least accurately represented my real life and instead proved to anyone bored enough to look that I was flawless in every way.

This meant posting pictures of not only me socializing with my super-huge group of friends, but also of my genetically, athletically, and educationally superior children, exotic Italian vacations, and Ryan Reynolds, my husband.

In addition, I had to produce photos of myself taken with soft focus from far enough away to appear as though I was ten years younger and a size two. Meaning someone had to snap them from across the Canadian border.

If that wasn't enough, I had to feign hobbies and interests, which I mostly made up like; I spend my free time running (to the grocery store). I love to travel (to and from school pickup). My favorite movie is *Twilight* (Okay, that one's true. Awkward).

But let's be honest right now. Who actually puts their normal life on social media? Like, if I was doing true status updates, I'd be posting things like, "Currently buying crap I don't need on Amazon because I have Prime" or "Watching *Dance Moms* and eating Ben & Jerry's Phish Food."

Beyond the wasting time thing, I also figured out pretty quickly that most everyone on Facebook falls into just a few categories: The Copious Poster, The Abundant Friender, The Voyeur, and My Aunt Mary.

Everyone knows a Copious Poster. Averaging new content about every three minutes, these folks never run out of pictures, comments, opinions, and inspirational quotes. There's nothing we don't know about them, from their kid's latest B+ to what time they brought the garbage out. I can't help but wonder if Copious Posters ever get anything done, hold down jobs, change clothes, or do anything other than hover over their mouse, waiting to share another Wine-O-Clock gif.

The Abundant Friender typically has at least 1,000 "friends," if not more. I'm pretty sure that I haven't even *met* that many people during the course of my entire life, let alone know them well enough to share the results of my most recent pap smear on the internet.

Then there's the Voyeur. They typically don't bother with profile pictures or personal information. They are there for one reason only, to scrutinize your stuff. They profess that they 'don't do' Facebook, but in reality, they spend more time doing it than everyone else combined.

This is evidenced by the fact that every time I meet up with one of my voyeur-friends, they have more dirt on my neighbors than a *Dateline* investigation.

And there's My Aunt Mary. Everyone has an Aunt Mary on Facebook. Enough said.

I did sign up for LinkedIn, or as I refer to it, Business Facebook. I only agreed to it because my dad insisted that it was CAREER SUICIDE not to. But I have yet to see a movie deal come through from one of my connections, and I'm not holding my breath.

I also caved and signed up for a Twitter account. I still don't get it and doubt that any of the four followers who read my irregular, rookie tweets do either.

By the time I actually figure it out, everyone will have

defected to Inane-Gram or whatever the next big thing is, anyway.

It doesn't matter. With 999,999,999 people out there, I'm fairly certain nobody is going to miss just one.

Is This Real Life?

I DON'T REALLY SPEND A WHOLE LOT OF TIME WATCHING VIDEOS on YouTube, but I still have a few favorites.

I really like the "Apparently Kid," "The Crazy Honey Badger," and the video where a couple of house cats negotiate a game of patty-cake while two guys do a voiceover of their supposed conversation.

It ends badly when one of the Pattycake Cats starts name-calling and the other admonishes "Dude, stop, just STOP, right now," resulting in a feline slap fight before it's all over.

My favorite, however, is "David After Dentist."

With more than 135 million views, the video is of a kid being filmed by his father after having a tooth extracted. Still loopy from the meds, the panicked seven-year-old asks all sorts of amusing philosophical questions, which I've decided parallel my experience of aging thus far.

At one point, a confused David asks his dad, "Is this real life?"

I sometimes wonder the same thing.

Recently I went to cook something on our kitchen stove, the one we've had for more than 12 twelve years, and reaching to turn on the front, right burner, I stopped and stared.

A dual-zone burner, it can be set to cook either a large or little pan, depending on which way you turn the knob.

Except there was no dual-zone burner.

Home alone, with no one around to assist me in what was rapidly becoming an existential crisis, I considered how, for more than a decade, I thought we had a dual-zone burner when it was clearly just a single.

I'm not sure how long I stood there, contemplating how many times I'd used the burner, what I'd cooked on it, why it looked so different, if it was "Berenstein" or "Berenstain" Bears, the meaning of life, if my doctor made house calls, before finally just accepting that there'd never been one in the first place and choosing another burner to heat up my frozen corn.

A couple days later, I became frustrated when, after trying to cook something on the front, right burner, I couldn't get the pan to heat up. I turned the knob up to the highest setting, still nothing.

It was then that I glanced down and realized that at some point, someone had taken all the knobs off, and put them back in the wrong places, including the dual-zone burner one, which was hiding in the back.

"Hon," I called to my husband, "Did you clean the stove?"

"Yes, why?" he replied.

There was no reason to respond that his errant knob relocation had me questioning reality and my place in the time-space continuum, or to ask why he was even cleaning the stove to begin with, since it wasn't Christmas or my birthday, so I didn't bother answering.

In the dentist video, an alarmed David tells his dad that he can't see anything, even though his eyes are open.

I can relate.

My kids like to point out that the text on my cell phone is set to a font so large that every message is like being yelled at, while also being visible to most orbiting satellites.

That's because at fifty-two, I now fall into the "Vision-Optional" category, where, no matter how hard I squint, I'm unable to perform some of life's most important tasks including ordering off a drink menu, checking the sale price, or reading the directions on a feminine moustache bleach kit.

"I feel funny," David says, "why is this happening to me?"

A fair question and one that also hits close to home.

Sometimes I find myself behind the wheel of my car, not sure where I'm going, why I'm going, or how I got there to begin with.

Not long ago, while driving to pick up one my daughters from visiting a friend, I missed an exit and drove clear to another state before realizing my mistake. On the return trip, I passed the same exact exit and drove an hour in the opposite direction before it dawned on me that I'd done it again.

Worse, I had my GPS on the entire time, but hadn't bothered consulting it, operating under the assumption that I didn't need it, because I knew where I was going.

Finally, before the dentist video ends, a defeated David asks his father if he's going to feel weird forever, to which his dad chuckles and assures him that it's only temporary.

I, unfortunately, will just have to wait and see.

Night at The Prom

EACH YEAR WHEN THE WEATHER WARMS UP AND THE JUNIORS section at Macy's becomes filled up with sparkly, sequined dresses, I reminisce about going to the prom.

I'm not ashamed to admit that if given the chance, I'd go again.

Not because I enjoyed any of the three times I went in high school.

In fact, just the opposite.

My first time was with a kid from a different town, who I'd met only once before at a keg party.

I must have made a good impression in my mullet and Duran Duran concert t-shirt, because not long after a friend of a friend's friend said he might be interested.

Even though the feeling wasn't mutual, I still said yes when he called and asked me to the prom.

Partly because I didn't know how to politely decline, but mostly because I wanted an excuse to dress up and get my hair done.

Taking full advantage of the opportunity, I promptly went out and bought a white gown so frilly that Scarlett O'Hara could've worn it to her first holy communion. The only thing missing was a hoop.

Paired with matching white, lace gloves and baby's breath in my upswept hair, I was the only bride in attendance that night.

I never saw my date again after that.

It's hard to say if it's because I gave him the "Let's Just Be Friends" speech when he brought me home, or because I'd used his junior prom as a trial run for my *Gone with the Wind*-inspired wedding.

The following year I was asked to prom by a semi-cool rocker kid I'd just started dating.

It might have all turned out alright, had I not decided to also start dating a kid I worked with at the local pharmacy.

And another kid I occasionally ran into when I was out underage drinking with my friends.

Like a real-life episode of The Bachelorette, I couldn't decide which one I liked more, so instead of choosing, I just went out with them all.

Not surprisingly, this didn't go over well. And one by one, they dumped me, including the rocker kid.

However, having already bought tickets and committed to a double date, we were still obligated to attend the prom.

Already less-than-ideal circumstances, the day before the big event I decided to 'tan' in the backyard for seven hours, char-broiling every free inch of real estate on my body.

The upside, however, is that I'd managed to find a prom dress custom-designed by Glenda the Good Witch (hoop included).

No crown was necessary; my hairdresser used an enormous hairpiece in creating my updo, making it appear as though a squirrel wearing copious amounts of Aqua Net had burrowed into the top of my head.

Still, it was a good time.

Rocker Kid and I didn't speak the entire night, the couple we'd gone with skipped out early (taking my resentful date with them), and I drove myself home at 9:30 p.m.

My final year of high school, I attended prom with my steady boyfriend at the time.

After the fiasco of the year before, I'd sworn off serial dating and settled down with my one, true love. My final, everlasting soul mate for the distance record of seven months.

Cash poor, I didn't have the funds for a new dress. Instead, I borrowed a used bridesmaid's dress from a friend.

Though it wasn't my first choice, it was the most perfect dress in the world – if my date was Wyatt Earp and the prom was being held at the Buckeye Saloon.

Outfitted in a burgundy, taffeta dress, accessorized with black lace stockings, lace gloves, and matching lace pillbox hat, I could've easily passed as Miss Kitty, right down to the black lace garter lassoed around my leg.

From what I remember, there were no gunslingers, wagon accidents or train robberies at the dance that night, making it the most successful of my three proms.

In hindsight, I've come to realize that my proms weren't nearly as bad as I remember.

They were worse.

But would I go again? In an instant.

Somewhere out there, there's a Disney princess dress, hoop-skirt and all, and it's calling my name.

Festivus for the Rest of Us

I LIKE HOLIDAYS.

My favorites are the ones that involve binge-eating while being showered with gifts, along with all occasions celebrated at someone else's house.

Regardless of the holiday, I'll celebrate it.

Even when there's not an occasion, I'll still celebrate it, provided dessert and gravy are served.

Fortunately, according to a list of U.S. holidays and observances, there are 250 special days commemorated in any given calendar year.

There are holidays for groundhogs, administrative professionals, employees, trees, taxes, pioneers, parents, senior citizens, and everything else shy of honoring spray deodorant.

Leif Erikson has his own holiday in October, though I can't understand why considering he only had a couple hit songs back in the '70s.

The Scots celebrate National Tartan Day in April. And while I'm really more of plaid person, I'm not opposed to a day of wearing skirts without underpants given the right circumstances.

Of the major holidays, my husband likes Thanksgiving the most. He says it's because it's relaxed and that we get to spend quality time with family.

I completely agree, of course, except for the "relaxed" and "quality time" parts.

Even though I don't usually host it, there's always some last-minute crisis with the dish I've volunteered to bring, like the time my husband helpfully offered to put my hash brown casserole in the oven.

A nice gesture if he'd remembered to remove the plastic covering first; a direct result of leaving him unsupervised in the kitchen.

With only minutes to spare before leaving, I pulled it out only to discover that instead of a casserole, my Thanksgiving contribution was Cling Wrap Cheesy Potatoes.

On the years that my side dish isn't a biohazard, someone has inevitably invited twenty-three extra guests to dinner at last minute, then complains that I didn't make enough.

And there's also the compulsory public speaking part when we go around the table and acknowledge what we're thankful for.

It's a tough crowd known to boo after the obligatory "I'm thankful for my friends and family," speech, which gives me performance anxiety when it's my turn.

If it were up to me, I'd skip the niceties and talk about stuff I'm actually thankful for like mixed drinks, Ped Egg refills on sale at CVS, and that the neighbor kids finally stopped chipping golf balls at our house when they think we're not home.

My favorite holiday is Halloween. The one time of year when it's not illegal to assume a fake identity and candy has no calories.

After that, it's probably Christmas. Even though it's at my house, I really enjoy it. Especially the moments right before people arrive and after they leave.

Other than that, it can be a little stressful.

First of all, no one ever comes on time.

There's always at least one Early-Arriver who shows up while we're still in a sweaty, pre-company vacuuming fugue, claiming I told them a different time than I actually did.

Worse, however, is the Late-Arriver, who pulls in just as everyone else is leaving. And with no place to be, becomes the Late-Stayer by default, parking it on the couch and opening another bottle of wine just when we think it's finally time for bed.

Most years there's also some kind of uncomfortable gift exchange.

For a long time, it was the Yankee Swap.

But year over year it grew increasingly contentious when it

became obvious that not everyone was sticking to the $25-per-gift plan.

Half of the contingency was re-gifting moldy items rummaged from the basement and the other half went over the top with lavish gifts in a shameless bid for favoritism.

With everyone fighting to secure the big-ticket items or dump the crap ones, it eventually turned into a hostile "Game of Thrones" situation, complete with sinister plots and backstabbing, all over a Dunkin' Donuts gift card.

One year, we tried celebrating the Seinfeld-inspired "Festivus."

While we didn't put up a silver pole, we did go out for Festivus Dinner at P.F. Chang's.

It started off well enough. Everyone was laughing and eating pot stickers until The Airing of Grievances started and things went downhill from there.

What began as a joke ended with no one speaking for the entire car ride home and we didn't celebrate Festivus again.

On the upside, there are only 319 days to go before Halloween.

And counting.

My Date with Oprah

I'VE HAD MY FAIR SHARE OF CELEBRITY ENCOUNTERS THROUGH the years.

Working as a production assistant at a news station, I once asked actress Fran Drescher if her New York accent was real, to which she leveled a look at me before drolly replying, "Do you really think I could make this up, honey?"

Back in the '80s, while working retail, I waited on members of the then-popular band, A-Ha. The hunky Norwegian lead singer needed jeans and when he came out of the fitting room to ask for a different size, he was only wearing underpants.

It was the seminal experience of my young life.

I met Oprah too. Kind of.

Late in the summer of 1994, I was a member of the Church of Oprah and like many other women, routinely planned my day around attending her 4:00 p.m. service. One afternoon while watching the show, an announcer came on and asked viewers to reach out if they wished their spouse could do something better like dance, cook, or be more romantic.

Having made a long-term career out of reading Harlequin romance novels, I eagerly penned a letter to Oprah explaining that my husband, the most wonderful person, like, *ever*, fell just a little short in the romantic-gesture department.

I was looking for long-stemmed roses, surprise trips to Paris, and jewelry in velvet boxes. All relatively reasonable requests.

Not wasting a moment, I dropped it in the mail.

It's hard to say how many letters the Oprah show received in those days, but if I had to guess, probably in the thousands. It came as a surprise, then, when one of Oprah's producers called a couple weeks later and invited us to be guests.

"I love your letter," he said. "We want you on the show."

All he needed, he said, were some photographs of our

kitchen and bedroom. Could I send some as soon as possible?

Breathless with excitement, I assured him that, oh yes, indeed, I could. *I was going to meet Oprah.*

Not long after hanging up, however, I began to feel uneasy.

While I had no problem going on national television to discuss my husband's romantic habits, convincing him that it was in his best interest to be globally shamed was going to be a tough sell.

I called him at work to share the good news and was met with silence.

When he finally spoke, he had a lot of questions. Sounding like someone negotiating a hostage release, he agreed to discuss it further when he got home.

Over dinner I cajoled, reassured, and promised that going on the Oprah show would be a wonderful experience.

Not seeing it, my husband remained reluctant and I was vaguely reminded of the time we thought our apartment was on fire and tried "saving" our cats by forcibly stuffing them into nylon gym bags.

As if on cue, the producer called back and after exchanging pleasantries with me, asked to speak with my husband.

I handed him the phone.

There were a few curt "yes's," some silence and then sounding puzzled my husband asked, "Pictures? Well, I'm not very comfortable with that. Okay. Yep. Goodbye."

And I knew my date with Oprah was over. I stared at him.

"He wanted pictures of our bedroom and kitchen," my husband said. "I wasn't comfortable with that, so we agreed that he should find another couple."

Eventually I got over it. Until I found out that the couple who took our place on the show was given an all new kitchen, complete with a champagne-stocked refrigerator, and bedroom furniture to boot.

A few years later, as a small consolation prize, I went to Chicago to watch a taping of the show.

Sitting in the audience, Oprah walked by on her way to the

set. It was my moment. Like a desperate teen at a One Direction concert, I stuck my hand out. I was going to meet Oprah. *No matter what.*

She looked down, and then at me, before reluctantly shaking it. In a huff, she marched away with a purpose that said some intern was about to be sacked for not having intervened.

I didn't really watch the show much after that.

Still. I met Oprah.

Granny Panties

I RECENTLY READ AN ARTICLE THAT SAID THONGS ARE ON THEIR way out and cotton, granny panties are making a comeback. I can't imagine why.

Personally, I think that thongs are, like, the way to go. Like most of my fifty-something friends, I find wearing cooking twine instead of traditional underwear to be almost as enjoyable as having dental X-Rays and suspicious moles removed.

I'm also worried about this latest fashion development because if they are phasing out thongs, what will they declare obsolete next? Metal corsets? Powdered wigs? *Hoop skirts*?

To be honest, up until a couple of years ago I thought thongs were the shoes you wear to beach, which is what we called them when I was a kid. I only realized my mistake when, while packing up sunscreen and towels, I told my daughters not to forget to bring their thongs and that I was already wearing mine.

The only other time I've ever seen them look that scared was when they found the "How Puppies Are Born" picture book in a box full of tag sale stuff at my sister-in-law's.

But, really, when you think about it, it's essentially the same principle.

Except that instead of plastic wedged uncomfortably between your first and second toes, it's scratchy lace wedged uncomfortably between…well, anyway, the good news is that I am already in style.

Most of my underpants already fall into the granny panty category and if, for the sake of fashion, I have to get rid of my extensive thong collection, I'm sure I can find a spare snack bag to hold them all. And I won't be sorry either.

I wasn't sorry when low-rise jeans fell out of favor. In fact, I was ecstatic to donate them after years of going out in public looking like a half-popped can of crescent dough and worrying that every time I bent over I was making history by broadcasting another lunar landing. One small bend for woman, one giant crevice exposed to mankind.

Fashion magazines say that "Mom" jeans are now back in style. When, exactly, did they go out? And what does that even mean? I have to assume, based on the name, that they are somewhat harried-looking, over-worked, under-appreciated, and on occasion they wet a tissue with their tongue to wipe something off your face. I probably won't wear them.

I guess anything is better than the trend I recently learned about called, 'Vajazzling.'

Operating under the same premise as the BeDazzler gadget that decorates your favorite jeans with beads and jewels, this spa treatment apparently embellishes something else entirely and has nothing to do with denim.

To be honest, most days I don't even feel like wearing earrings, let alone a complete disco ball display under my clothes.

I'd consider doing it once a year just to give my gynecologist a little break in the regular action. Before starting I could announce loudly, "And now for something completely different!" Or, "I seem to have developed an unusual rash, can you take a look?"

But it's unlikely. I barely made it through a bikini wax recently.

First of all, it hurt so much that I screamed like an elementary schoolgirl in the middle of a dodgeball match. I couldn't even look when it was done fearing that instead of hair removal, I'd just undergone a skin graft without anesthetic and needed immediate medical attention.

More importantly, it was administered by same woman who's been painting my nails for the last ten years. I realized afterward that once the line between trimming cuticles and pouring burning wax on the inside of someone's legs then ripping it off with duct tape has been crossed, there's really no going back.

She still paints my nails, but neither of us makes eye contact. That's okay. Now that granny panties are back in fashion, there's a lot less visible real estate for me to worry about and I probably won't need to do it again. If I want to go to the beach, I can just wear shorts. And my thongs.

Paper Ass

To look at me you probably wouldn't guess that most days I've emptied out my considerable arsenal of profane words before spooning sugar into my second cup of coffee.

It's an unfortunate character flaw. One that doesn't exactly gel with my carefully cultivated Playgroup Mom persona, but lurks just beneath the surface waiting for any excuse to erupt like a hot, dumpster fire.

I can only assume it's something I inherited from my parents along with clacking ankle bones and the ability to appear as though I'm actually listening when other people talk.

Growing up, my dad, in particular, had a colorful vocabulary. One that he liberally used in every possible scenario.

In fact, he invoked both God and Jesus so much during my childhood, that when it comes time to meet them, I'm pretty sure they'll be waiting for him with a clipboard and transfer orders.

While there was always some legitimate reason for him to break out his impressive collection of NC-17 phrases, like not being able to find a spoon in the dishwasher or discovering that I'd eaten the last of his Jell-O Pops, it was in the car where he did his most inspired work.

Pensive, with a rigid grip on the steering wheel, anything could set him off. A tailgater, someone not paying attention, a random car pulling out, were all incentives for an angry, spit-laced, tirade.

But mostly it was anyone going too slow in front of him that provoked acute episodes of binge swearing.

With my brother and I sitting in the back seat, he'd sometimes attempt to keep it family-friendly by uttering "C'mon, you turkey."

But that was rare.

Typically, he used longer, more offensive phrases which increased exponentially depending on how long we were stuck behind the driver and just how slow they were traveling.

It was like attending an educational seminar on road rage with live demonstrations.

Occasionally, he'd get creative and make up entirely new swear words. To this day my personal favorite remains, "Paper Ass," said with each syllable drawn out for effect.

Paaaaayy-Perrrr Aaaaaaasssssssss

I seriously have no idea what it means.

I can only assume it implies that the motorist in question is somehow equipped with a butt so wispy and easily crumpled up, that it's physically impossible for them to drive anywhere close to the speed limit.

I should also point out that my dad wasn't the only offender in the household. Though far less frequent, my mom had her moments as well.

Once, while standing directly in front of an open window, she lost her mind trying to attach a vacuum hose to the canister, yelling out a string of profanities explicit enough to make George Carlin blush, only to look up and discover the UPS guy standing frozen outside.

Without another word she signed for her package, then closed the window.

Then there's me.

A considerable amount of restraint has been necessary during the last couple of decades as my kids have been growing up. It's important to me that they not think their mom is some kind of trash-talking, boozy sailor, even though most nights by around 6:30 p.m. that's pretty much what they've got anyway.

Now that they're older, my resolve has loosened. Most everything I say includes at least a couple curses and usually it's because the spoon I'm looking for is missing from the dishwasher or someone has eaten the last of my Edy's ice cream.

It's gotten so bad that I find it necessary to replay conversations in my head, doublechecking that I haven't accidently dropped the F-bomb while discussing the latest Mary Higgins Clark novel with my mother-in-law.

The good news is that, thanks to my husband, I don't have to worry about making up my own swear words.

For my birthday he gifted me, "Creative Cursing: A Mix and Match Profanity Generator."

It's a flip book that allows you to combine any number of curses into new variations in order to avoid redundancy and it really comes in handy when I've used up all of mine.

Not surprisingly, however, paper ass is nowhere to be found.

The Sports Gene

GROWING UP, OUR NEIGHBORS HAD A SMALL DUCK POND THAT, once frozen in the winter, became my personal skating rink. Sometimes after school I'd walk over, shovel off the snow, and work on my short program.

It was exactly the same as the one Alexis Winston did in *Ice Castles* when she wore the pretty, blue skating dress that gruff-but-kindhearted Coach Beulah had specially embroidered with her name on the collar. But, after she became famous, Lexie was too embarrassed to wear it. She wore it again when she finally pulled off the triple axel despite being blind and tripping over the flowers at the end. Roll credits.

The only difference is that my routine didn't include any spins, flips, jumps, loops, Lutzes, Salchows, Camels, lifts, or anything other than a few wobbly passes around the ice. Sometimes there was some unplanned backwards skating resulting in a massive wipeout, before wrapping up practice for the day.

When I eventually realized that I was never going to be chosen for the Olympics, let alone medal, I turned my attention to my other passion; gymnastics.

With no formal training, instruction or a single gymnastics class under my belt, I went out for the sport in middle school.

Oh sure, I had spent countless hours in our front yard nailing down a forward roll, but my cartwheel needed serious work and I'd never even heard of a back handspring, let alone a vault.

That didn't stop me. I just assumed that the coach would teach me everything I needed to know.

I was surprised, then, when Ms. Bothwell (also my unforgiving gym teacher), dismissed me on the first day with nothing more than a bewildered look before moving on to instruct the other girls who already knew how to do all sorts of gravity-defying tumbles and didn't appear to need the least bit of help with any of them.

Discouraged, I ended up quitting, but not before competing in a regional meet first. After seeing my lame-duck name on the roster, the judges threatened to disqualify the team if I didn't do my floor exercise, which wouldn't have been so bad, if I'd had one.

Instead, for ninety glacial seconds, I ran wildly along the mats, improvising faux-ballet leaps and jumps, while adding a couple of somersaults for good measure, until the final notes of "If I Were a Rich Man" (the instrumental version), blared out from the speakers.

From what I remember, no one clapped when it was over, and the judges' score was lower than the daily interest earned on my checking account.

The following year I tried out for the school band color guard. There were 10 spots and 12 of us trying out. It was an intense battle of marching and flag-spinning. When the dust settled, 10 lucky girls had been chosen, along with one alternate, leaving me as the only one who didn't make the cut, effectively ending any future aspirations to do a sport of any kind.

Not much has changed since becoming an adult. Throughout the years I've attempted to improve my abysmal athletic skills but without much success.

I tried Zumba a few years ago and was the one person mamboing to the right while everyone else was doing the salsa to the left. Instead of executing steamy Latin dance moves, my awkward dancing looked more like I was trying to hail a cab during rush hour or learning how to swim after accidentally falling into the deep end.

For added measure, the large floor-to-ceiling mirrors in the studio revealed things about myself that I didn't necessarily want to know, like the Rockettes can rest easy knowing there's one less person in the world competing for their job. And that stretch pants only look good from the front.

The upside is that I recently read an article saying scientists have discovered a special gene that athletes and other sporty people are apparently born with, enabling them to do more than sweat and mouth-breathe while walking the treadmill at its lowest setting.

If true, I'm pretty sure that it explains why other people can do stuff like ski and play volleyball, while my abilities are limited to laundry-changing and getting the mail without breaking a leg.

It also lets me off the hook. The winter Olympics are coming up and my short program needs a lot of work.

The Insomniac Sleep Club for Women

I'VE DECIDED THAT MOST PEOPLE FALL INTO ONE OF TWO CATE-gories. Those who can sleep and everybody else. No exceptions.

I find that the sleepers of the world are oddly pleased with their borderline narcolepsy and cheerfully fill non-sleepers in on their ability to sleep anytime, anywhere. No matter what.

In addition, they don't mind sharing that they average twelve hours most nights and that they'd sleep even more if there wasn't a pressing reason to get up, like a job, basic hygiene require-ments, or an overactive bladder.

As a member of the Insomniac Sleep Club for Women, I harbor a fair amount of resentment and loathing for these peo-ple and their excessive sleep.

My husband is one of them.

When we were first married, I can remember earnestly con-fessing all my hopes and desires into the wee hours of the night, only to realize that he hadn't made it past "I always dreamed of being an ice dancer" before nodding off. I just assumed he was a good listener.

In a remarkable display of snooze aptitude, he can sleep through just about anything including most airline flights regardless of what's happening.

Mouth open and head bouncing around on a crescent roll neck pillow, he's been known to blithely slumber away as flight attendants frantically run to their seats, overhead bins are spill-ing open, and the plane is performing air show stunts flying through bad weather.

Meanwhile, sitting beside him, bathed in sweat, I'm praying the Rosary and scribbling last goodbyes on a peanut napkin.

Once, when our house alarm went off in the middle of the night, my husband stumbled out of bed, shut it off, and got back under the covers. Rigid with terror, I hissed, "What are you *doing?* The alarm is going off!"

It took a few moments of him squinting at me, attempting to remember how we were related, before he was finally conscious enough to realize that something was wrong.

It was good to note that had Freddy Krueger broken in and stuffed me into the woodchipper instead of someone accidentally leaving the basement door slightly ajar, my husband would have slept through the entire thing.

I've noticed that sleepers also seem to have uncanny ability to immediately return to sleep if they are woken up as if nothing ever happened.

For someone like me, however, a Honda Civic backing out of a driveway one town over will jolt me awake and I'm up for rest of the night.

Sometimes I don't mind, it gives me a chance to catch up on the latest infomercials.

Who buys this stuff?

I've never seen any of it advertised during the day. They must cater strictly to the red-eye demographic assuming that only those suffering from acute sleep deprivation would ever consider purchasing the craptactular assortment of items being hawked.

I'll admit, however, that in the predawn hours, I am vulnerable. At times I've been nearly convinced that I can't live without a food vacuum sealer that will convert my leftover pot roast into birthday gifts.

And Christy and Chuck have nearly persuaded me that a Total Gym, with all its versatile settings, is exactly what I need to be featured in the next Sports Illustrated Swimsuit Edition. As a bonus, it slides under the bed for storage, which is where it would remain after a single use until exhumed by archeologists.

I've also learned that if I want to be a teenager again, I need only to invest in the Tai Cheng video for seniors.

In just ninety days, I'll have fewer aches and pains, more

balance, agility, and if I play my cards right, a real shot at competing at Wimbledon.

Sure, there have been a handful of times that I've really been tempted to buy something. Once, I had my credit card out and was prepared to order the magic Nutribullet until realizing that it's only for making smoothies.

Lying awake in the middle of the night, I try to imagine what it's like to be a sleeper. But since I'll probably never know, I just pull my Snuggie closer and dream of all the money I'm going to make using my new real estate videos.

The Gum Accident

IF I WERE A SUPERHERO, I'D BE "CAPTAIN AWKWARD" FOR MY extraordinary ability to turn the most mundane situations into embarrassing ones.

Once, at a crowded deli counter, I patiently waited for my turn to order. When the clerk called my number, I loudly announced that I wanted two, large breasts. The moment I realized what I'd said, I felt everyone's eyes on me, and a small giggle escaped. The more I attempted to clarify that I had actually meant chicken breasts, the harder I laughed.

The fact the no one else laughed with me only fueled the situation and with tears running down my face, I ended up leaving and getting takeout instead.

There was also the time I gave the whole "Scan-n-Bag" your own groceries thing a try. While checking out, I innocently asked the clerk how they prevented people from just sticking stuff into their bags without paying. The clerk looked up and studied me, and I then realized that she was contemplating whether or not I'd filled up mine with enough unscanned pine nuts and saffron to send my kids to college.

Prickly heat crept up the back of my neck and my face turned magenta. I looked guiltier than the time it was all quiet in the movie theater and I told my husband that it was just my stomach.

I'm pretty sure there's a picture of me hanging on the bulletin board in the break room and I don't ever try and scan my own groceries anymore.

In addition to routinely humiliating myself, my other superpower is making unfortunate choices.

Being one of those people who compulsively records every moment of their kids' lives, I had my husband videotape me without a single stitch of clothing when I was nine months pregnant with our second daughter.

As if at any point in the future we'd sit down as a family in front of the TV, make popcorn, and watch me parade around naked, looking like a python that swallowed a Toyota.

Of course, after a couple of moves, I lost the tape and have spent the past 18 years paralyzed with fear that in the event of my death, some unsuspecting family member will pop it in a VCR thinking they are about to watch a Girl Scout pinning ceremony and discover something else entirely.

If I'm the Batman of embarrassment and unfortunate choices, my mom is Robin. A few years back she went on a lunch date with a male friend at an upscale restaurant. Shortly after being seated, she excused herself to use the ladies' room.

After settling into a stall, she wadded up some toilet paper to have on deck for when she finished. While waiting, she absently took out the gum that she'd been chewing, stuck it in her reserve, then forgot.

A few moments later, however, she was acutely reminded.

Though most women's bathrooms have vending machines for various feminine emergencies, very few, if any, dispense jars of peanut butter in the event of an unexpected gum accident.

Immobilized, my mom sat there attempting to figure out proper protocol for what amounted to a sticky situation. Given its location, removing the gum was complicated. But leaving things as they stood wasn't an option either.

After fifteen minutes, her worried date sent someone in to look for her. Too embarrassed to admit that she had a stick of chewed-up Trident stuck in the world's most inconvenient place, she simply called out "I'm okay," before finally managing to pick out enough of the gum to return to the table and finish the date.

As sort of a PSA, my mom agreed to let me share her story so that others might learn from her experience and avoid the inherent dangers that come with multitasking in a public restroom.

After hearing her story, I nearly stopped chewing gum altogether.

But I've got bigger problems. There's a missing videotape and I'm not sure how much time I've got left to find it.

The Book of Love

Like Indiana Jones and the Holy Grail, I recently came across a literary masterpiece buried beneath a Partridge Family record and some dead spiders in my basement: *The Book of Love*.

It wasn't authored by Shakespeare, Lord Byron, or even E. L. James, author of *Fifty Shades of Grey* (which I discovered isn't actually about love or choosing a new paint color for my living room, like, *at all*).

Nope. *The Book of Love* was written by a wordsmith of the highest caliber, one with such a commanding knowledge of romance and gift for prose that if Danielle Steel were to read it, she'd never write another "moving and emotionally-charged" novel, ever again.

Scrawled in poorly executed cursive, the manuscript's opening lines are at once both gripping and powerful.

Well, today is my 13th birthday. I'll try and write in here every day. Carie is the best friend a kid could have. P.S. I still like Craig.

Beginning in May of 1981, my diary chronicles what could arguably be one of the most definitive case studies on Love and the Hormonal Adolescent ever documented.

For the better part of six years I wrote about a litany of "best" friends who came and went more frequently than seasonal allergies. I wrote about how much I loved my parents, when I didn't hate them. I wrote about the usual trials and tribulations of school. But, far and away, more than anything else, I wrote about just one thing.

Love.

Based on my diary, I fell in love more times than a Mass Pike tollbooth spits out tickets on St. Patrick's Day.

There was Craig, Gary, Steve, Wayne, Jim, Bob, Doug, Todd, Pete, Bruce, Erik, Chad, Blair, Nathan, Paul, Pat, Chuck, Blaine, Jay, Joel, Bill and enough others to publish a 1,001 Baby Names book.

There were also a handful of special guest stars that made reoccurring appearances for months, sometimes years at a time.

Among them was Scott, my middle school crush who, in hindsight, was a deplorable, offensive kid who made inappropriate comments in my general direction, which I misinterpreted as mutual attraction.

It didn't matter. I *loved* him.

So much, in fact, that I filled up pages with our someday married names and pressed flowers in my diary with florid poems to accompany them.

Dearest Scott. I place this flower to remember you to me. Just a constant reminder of how much I love thee. When you smile, it makes my day. When you cup my chin and look into my eyes, I feel very okay.

I love Scott so much. I hear he's gonna ask me out. Oh God, I can't wait. I love him. Oh, please, Scott, ask me out.

Scott did not ask me out.

Then there was Sean. He was my best friend's cousin and the true marquee headliner.

During the prolific "Sean Years" I listened to Air Supply songs around the clock and spent endless nights crying in my pillow.

I just got off the phone with Sean. Something has definitely changed between us. When he called me Babe, he was serious. God, I really wanted to say that "I love you, Sean and I hope you feel the same, my love."

Another day spent thinking about Sean. He called last night. I wasn't home. I wish I had been home. I got a perm today.

Sean? Sean, who? Oh, you mean the one who broke my heart tonight? Yeah, I know him. I wasn't hurt that he's going out with Nicole, I always cry like that. How is it the day after pain? I'm surviving and letting the word "care" slip obsequiously from my vocabulary, except to say, "I don't care."

In five years, we never actually went out. Also, I used the word "obsequiously."

Maybe the biggest irony of all is that the first page of my old diary comes with a printed inscription written by poet, Henry Wadsworth Longfellow that reads, "My own thoughts are my companions."

After reading the *Book of Love* from cover to cover, I disagree. My thoughts were anything but my companions. Instead they went by the names of Craig, Gary, Steve, Wayne, Bob, Doug, Todd…

Lady of Athleisure

I'M A LITTLE SLOW ON THE UPTAKE WHEN IT COMES TO FASHION.
Just when I finally got used to low-rise, boot cut jeans, high-waisted, skinny legs came back in style, leaving me confused over whether I'm required to continue emphasizing my ample waistline or switch to accentuating my cankles.

I also completely missed the entire puffy coat revolution, as it's made a huge comeback.

I just assumed that it was an outdated holdover from my childhood when everyone dressed up for winter as the Michelin Man, complete with moonboots, which, if we're being honest here, remain fashion's greatest accomplishment to date.

Foamy, squishy, and decidedly modern with their bright colors and stripes, I'd still wear them today given the opportunity. Especially if I were selected to help colonize Mars, because, after all, that's what they were designed for.

Then again, I'd also leave the house dressed like Boy George if I didn't think the employees at Stop & Shop would look at me more strangely than they already do.

Styles were pretty cool back in the '80s. Other than donning a top hat and ribbon-entwined braids, my favorite look was combining a pair of black stretch pants with a giant, neon sweater that forgave all the sins committed by late night Domino's pizza delivery. Even if it did make me look like a construction sign.

From what I understand, stretch pants are again back in fashion, but rebranded as "leggings," because calling them "stretch pants" sounds about as sexy as buying orthopedic shoes for the prom.

Unlike the first time around, people now wear them with crop-tops and form-fitting pullovers.

Apparently by choice.

If you ask me, it's a direct violation of the stretch-pant

concept, which dictates they be coupled with an oversized shirt as to suggest that hiding underneath is a very fit, diminutive person, without actually having to be one.

Now, instead of camouflaging trouble spots, they're intended to enhance them, and more than that, the wearer is actually supposed to look *good* in them, defeating the purpose altogether.

Stretch pants aside, not long ago, I noticed an increasing number of people wearing athletic clothes in restaurants, at social events, even the grocery store and was instantly threatened by it.

Who were these extremists, exercising so excessively that they had no choice but to wear their workout clothes in public? And more important, how dare they show off their dedication to physical fitness, making me feel inadequate just because I prefer hibernating to hiking?

Soon after, I began seeing exercise clothes crop up at all my favorite stores, usually next to the puffy coat section, leading me to believe that not only was everyone kayaking or rock-climbing during their lunch breaks, but preparing for the next ice age as well.

After months of bemoaning a world filled with cold, but healthy, zealots, it finally dawned on me that far from working out, these people were simply wearing the latest fashion: Athleisure.

Once I realized that wearing Lycra in public was not only acceptable, but highly fashionable, I dropped my donut and headed straight for the mall.

Despite attempting to look like all the other stylish women outfitted in sleek leggings, fancy running shoes, ponytails, and shiny vests, my athleisure ensembles fell short, looking more like I just crawled out of bed, than just finished doing crunches with my trainer.

Maybe I just picked out all the wrong things.

More likely, it's because my overall aesthetic indicates that the only physical activity I'm capable of performing is emptying the dishwasher; a reasonably accurate assumption.

Either way, I continue searching for suitable athleisure as I, too, would like to look like I pretend to exercise, just like everyone else.

Or maybe I'll hire an athleisure stylist, someone who can help me successfully dress in the clothes I occasionally sweat in, without looking like I actually did.

But chances are, by the time I finally figure out how to wear puffy coats and athleisure, the fashion world will have already moved on to the next big thing, which, God-willing, will include ribbon-entwined braids and top hats.

I've got my fingers crossed.

It's Still Good

THE SINGLE QUESTION I AM ASKED MOST OFTEN BY MY HUSBAND and kids, surprisingly, is not, "Would you like another foot rub?"

Or, "What are you going to do with all your free time?"

And definitely not "How would you like us to arrange the decorative pillows on the couch?"

No, the most popular inquiry in my house is a simple one. "Is this still good?"

Apparently, determining whether something in the refrigerator has gone from edible to toxic waste dump, is a task that I, alone, am capable of performing, along with cleaning up cat vomit, and figuring out what to have for dinner.

Considering my husband works a complex technology job, has constructed a small computer empire in our basement, and can assemble Ikea furniture, it seems implausible that when it comes to perishables, he's unable to distinguish between bologna and botulism.

Yet, I often find him nervously contemplating leftover pizza, vacillating between potential starvation or certain death. Paralyzed with indecision, I'm his only hope.

"Is this still good?"

My kids are no different.

Both are midway through college, and neither knows how to make an appointment, add bleach to the whites, or communicate in person, let alone navigate the confusing process of inspecting something before deciding to eat it.

Not long ago, one daughter finished an entire bowl of cereal before realizing that the milk she'd used had long since gone bad.

While I'm no rocket scientist, I am capable of identifying yogurt, and would certainly know to avoid it, if dumped all over my Cheerios.

That's probably because I have PTSD after growing up in a

family where everything was "still good," regardless of whether it actually was or not.

As a kid, the openly-flaming bread my mom had forgotten under the broiler, was still good, even if it was charred and smoldering on the cookie sheet.

The Five-Second Rule was closer to the Five-to-Ten-Minute-Maybe-Even-Longer Rule, because if you could wipe it off, or rinse it in the sink, it was still good, no matter how much hair was stuck to it.

And it wasn't uncommon to pop open Mrs. Butterworth's yellow head and pour syrup laced with furry, Petri dish specimens onto my Eggos, which is how I knew that it wasn't, actually, still good.

But, being too lazy to throw it out, I just put it back, figuring someone else would take care it.

Eventually, after years of being cross-examined over how old something in the refrigerator was, my mom reflexively responded, "It's still good," when she heard the door open, even when no one asked.

I'm pretty sure, however, it's not only my family that blatantly ignores common food sense.

On a warm summer day a few years back, we went to my mother-in-law's for dinner. As an appetizer, she set out crackers and a nut-encrusted cheese ball.

Remembering a similar one she'd served at Christmas, I asked how she'd managed to find another.

"Oh, it's the same one," she breezily replied, "I just cut off the bad parts. It's still good."

Much like the Cheese Ball Policy, my in-law's Wine Policy governs that any opened bottle of wine has a shelf life of infinity.

While I agree that it's okay to drink spoiled wine under the right circumstances (family gatherings, post-school open houses, and 5:00 p.m.), I draw the line at something that was uncorked in a different calendar year since, generally speaking, I prefer my balsamic in salad dressing, as opposed to a glass.

I can only assume that, because many foods are, in fact,

perishable, this is why manufacturers provide expiration dates, a courtesy indicating that, once passed, we shouldn't eat them unless seeking a free colonic or extended vacation in the ER.

And sure, sometimes it's fine to go a few days beyond that date, depending on the item's overall odor, color, and appearance, just so long as it's not "still good" based solely on desire, instead of fact.

Recently, in an attempt to teach my husband and kids some basic life skills should they ever have to eat in my absence, when they ask if something is still good, I've started replying, "Do *you* think it's still good?"

Most of the time they respond by staring at me, trying to gauge if I'm serious, before giving up, and putting it back in the refrigerator.

We've got a long way to go.

A Christmas to Remember

PEOPLE ARE OFTEN SURPRISED WHEN THEY LEARN HOW CLOSE I once came to being a superstar.

Of course, looking at me now, it's probably easier to imagine that I was on the fast track to do something in relativistic quantum field theory or at the very least, multivariable calculus. But no. I was headed for the big time.

My brush with fame occurred when I was eleven and appeared in a made-for-TV movie with Joanne Woodward.

Through a series of events too long-winded to explain without turning into that friend who monopolizes dinner with stories you don't want to hear but are stuck listening to anyway, my brother and I were invited to be extras in a 1978 film called, *A Christmas to Remember.*

With a cast including Joanne, Jason Robards, and Eva Marie Saint, it was a weepy tale about city parents who can no longer care for their son during the Great Depression and send him to live with his grandparents on a farm in the Midwest.

After filming most of the movie in rural Minnesota, our scene was being shot in a Minneapolis alley with Woodward delivering the bad news to her son that he's being sent away.

The night before we were due to arrive on set, my mom took my brother and me to a local secondhand store to find clothes suited to our starring turns as Street Kids One and Two, because, as it turns out, they didn't wear plaid bell bottoms in the 1930's.

And, also, because there apparently wasn't enough extra cash in the CBS Movie of the Week budget for additional wardrobe.

I was heady with anticipation. A thespian to the core, I had appeared in several Kennedy Elementary School shows, including a performance as Lead Cowboy in the summer school production of Jessie James and jingle bell ringer for "Up on the

Rooftop," during the holiday chorus concert.

But this was going to be my big break; I just knew it.

Soon after we arrived, my brother was assigned the scene-stealing role of Boy-With-Hands-In-Pockets, while I, along with one other extra, was to be a Hopscotch Girl.

Take after take, I threw my stone and hopped perfectly in hopes of being the best Hopscotch Girl director George Englund had ever seen.

When the cameras weren't rolling, I stood close to Joanne and the other A-listers chatting on set, hoping they'd stop and suddenly realize that standing among them was the next Jodie Foster or Kristy McNichol. I even lounged in Joanne's director's chair until a crew member caught me and booted me out.

When the long day of filming was over, I went home satisfied. I had done some networking, laid down my finest hopscotch, and was sure that once my scene appeared on television, I'd be fending off casting calls.

So convinced of my imminent celebrity status, I bragged about my upcoming feature film debut to just about everyone who'd listen, including all the "friendly" farm kids on my hour-long bus ride to and from school.

Preferring penny loafers to bib overalls and Broadway tunes to chicken feed, it's fair to say that I wasn't really their type. Even so, I craved their acceptance and hoped that my meteoric rise to fame would finally earn it.

The movie aired a few days before Christmas. My family gathered around the TV and waited for the big moment when my brother, Hands-in-Pockets, would appear and I would shine as Hopscotch Girl.

We watched in stunned humiliation when it became obvious that my brother's work had ended up on the cutting room floor, and mine, while still in the film, was a fleeting image of a blurred figure lasting less than a nanosecond on the screen. Even worse, Hopscotch Girl II was standing in front of me, blocking my shot.

I waited in dread for the school bus the next morning.

As I did the walk of shame up down the aisle, the silence was deafening, and no one would push in so that I could sit with them.

After a few minutes of crickets, I heard some kid mutter, "Good job in the movie," and I knew my career was over.

A Christmas to Remember is listed on IMDB. It's got ninety-seven good ratings and includes a list of the cast. I'm thinking about adding my name and picture.

It's not too late.

The Travel Games

RIGHT UP FRONT, I ADMIT THAT ANY TRIP WITH MY HUSBAND and kids inevitably becomes some combination of *The Hunger Games* and the Dr. Phil show. Whoever who makes it to the end, without being killed off by one of the other three, wins. Or at the very least, requires serious therapy.

Despite knowing this, I still planned a two-week family trip to Europe eight years ago.

It started off well enough. We visited castles, rode gondolas, and took pictures of each other holding up the Leaning Tower of Pisa. No one minded that there was a sweeping heatwave which made everything feel as though we were competing in a decathlon held on the end of a blowtorch.

We laughed when there was no ice in our drinks, seats on the toilets, air conditioners in our hotel rooms, or screens in the windows. We were in Europe! Ciao! Prego! Guten Tag! LOL!

Things began to unravel when my husband forgot to program the GPS and we drove seventy miles in the wrong direction before figuring it out and nearly had a full-blown domestic incident on the autobahn.

Then, during a breathtaking hike along the Mediterranean coastline, my fourteen-year-old, or as we call her "The Weakest Link," spent five of the six miles plaintively asking if she could go home, or at the very least, text, while our sixteen-year-old walked with another tour group entirely and pretended not to know us.

Ultimately, it was the hurricane that proved to be our demise.

Sure, we'd been following the news. But it wasn't until frenzied reporters on The Weather Channel began predicting that the entire east coast was going to break apart like a pie crust and fall into the ocean that we panicked.

Partly, it was because our flight back to the states was the same day Hurricane Irene was expected to hit. But mostly it was that, deep down, we all understood that if we were trapped together in a foreign country for any further length of time, not all of us would be returning.

Sitting in a Rome hotel room at midnight, rivulets of sweat running down my back, I listened to our airline's looped, midi-keyboard hold music for three straight hours before the call center randomly disconnected me.

I've never been closer to needing the services of a criminal defense attorney in my entire life.

After a second attempt, I finally reached an agent who could only find a lone flight to Chicago. Despite living in Connecticut, we took it.

The airport looked like one of those disaster movie scenes where everyone is trying to get out of the city with all their earthly possessions. There were throngs of sweaty people, excessive luggage, and a one-legged pigeon hopping around.

Our seats on the plane weren't together. My husband, the lottery winner, sat somewhere in the front, while my daughters and I were assigned to the very last seats, in the very last row, directly next to the bathrooms.

It was like being locked in the trunk of a car for eleven hours with 250 people, all suffering from some form of Marco Polo's revenge.

Upon arriving in Chicago, my husband went for the luggage and we got McDonald's. Like animals, the three of us ate in huge bites without speaking. Dragging four suitcases, my husband came back just in time to watch his bag of food dump over and spill out on the airport floor. We averted our eyes and kept eating. No one was going to share.

In a rental car that cost more than our mortgage, we drove straight through without stopping.

After days without bathing, we arrived home smelling of gym shoes and hot cheese only to discover there was no power or water. After fermenting for a couple more, my mother-in-law called to say that their power had been restored and that we could come over to shower.

There were no lights on when we pulled in. Apologetically she explained that she had mistaken the sun reflecting on their digital clock to mean that the power was back on. It wasn't.

To this day, I wonder if she realizes just how close we were to teaching her a lesson about how electricity works.

In hindsight, it's all pretty funny and we can laugh about it now. I think it's because the four of us made it back to tell the story. Depending on what happens the next time, someone might not be so lucky.

Close Encounters of the Alien Kind

My parents aren't very social people.

I surmise this from the fact that when I was still in pre-school, they fled the bustling Minneapolis suburb we lived in and relocated in an area of southeastern Minnesota so remote, the closest town was a long-distance phone call away.

And just to ensure that we were completely isolated, like an Artic research camp, they built their home on eight, heavily-wooded acres, far from of any type of human interaction or modern conveniences like paved roads and electricity.

Had the Unabomber settled there, they'd still be searching for him.

For much of my childhood I enjoyed a daily, hour-long bus ride to and from school where I learned many of life's important lessons, like metal Scooby-Doo lunchboxes hurt when they make contact with the back of your head. And when the parochial schoolgirls stick half-eaten candy canes in the hood of your coat, they aren't trying to share.

Winter typically arrived between Columbus Day and Halloween, and there was even one year that nearly three feet of snow fell on Halloween and didn't melt until May. But it really didn't matter since our location essentially rendered trick-or-treating obsolete.

Apparently, that whole deal only works if you've got neighbors.

But I give my mom credit for trying. Each year at about 5:30 p.m. on Halloween, she would suddenly remember that it was, in fact, Halloween and scramble to find something other than instant coffee and croutons to throw into the pumpkin bucket of some obviously lost child or Survivorman, the only two people capable of finding our house.

She'd miraculously discover uneaten candy from the previous

Easter in the back of a drawer, insist it was still good, and deliver it along with a handful of change from my dad's nightstand as if to say, "Hey kid, take this and buy yourself some real candy."

Because we'd forgotten to get a costume, I'd rummage through stinky boxes of old clothes in the basement looking for something that I could use. One year my mom's slightly mildew-stained white dress transformed me into a "bride." Another year an errant gold earring and an ascot tied to my head served as my "gypsy" get-up.

Once I procured a costume, (or dirty clothes by any other name) my mom would drive me to nearest town/outpost where she'd drop me off in some unsuspecting neighborhood. There I'd frantically dash from house to house trying to maximize my net intake before she honked, signaling that it was time to go home.

It wouldn't have been so bad if I didn't have to also trick-or-treat for my brother, who had to stay home because he was too sick to trick-or-treat himself.

That would have been okay had he actually been sick, instead of just too old and lazy to go out.

But since he was unwilling to forgo a pillowcase full of candy, I was coerced under the threat of bodily harm to ask for extra candy at every house, enduring suspicious looks from homeowners who, based on what I was wearing, weren't sure if I was there to trick-or-treat or steal garden tools from their backyard.

Eventually, however, karma found my brother.

Throughout the years, various friends and extended family members had speculated that our remote setting provided the ideal location for an alien landing.

Having seen every alarming UFO movie of the 1970's, including *Close Encounters of the Third Kind*, aliens showing up at our house not only seemed like a distinct possibility, but a foregone conclusion.

Because of this, neither my brother nor I slept for the better part of nine years. Instead we spent most nights staring at the ceiling in abject terror waiting to be abducted by creatures with long arms and sightless black eyes.

On the night they arrived, my brother awoke to the sound of someone softly pinging the strings of my mother's old banjo, which sat in the corner of his room. Paralyzed by fear, he lay helpless to do anything but wait for the light to beam him up to the awaiting ship.

When it didn't happen, he eventually sprinted to the light switch only to discover that the aliens were, in fact, just a single wood roach meandering up the banjo strings.

It would be another nine years before he slept again.

Promptly after high school, I moved to the nearest big city where I stayed until having children of my own, and then retreated to a small town that seemed like a good place to raise them.

It's semi-rural, but we have neighbors within earshot, local calls are free, and I'm pretty sure there's not a single place to land a spacecraft.

Burn, Baby, Burn

I LOVE SUMMER. FOR A SHORT, BLISSFUL TIME, I DON'T REQUIRE fleece-lined underpants, or the thermostat set to "incinerate" to maintain a body temperature above my usual meat locker. I guess that explains why I also love going to the beach.

With line-of-sight to the sun, I spend most weekends splayed on the sand like a reptile wearing orange Lycra in a futile attempt to heat my blood up enough to withstand another year.

However, beach days don't come without a price.

Each June, I'm forced to acknowledge that I haven't done a single thing to take care of myself in any of the preceding nine months. Then before trying on my summer clothes, I find religion and pray that something still fits after a winter of eating everything that wasn't nailed down.

Pulling on shorts for the first time, I am instantly suspicious that my neighbors have been supplying the History Channel with that grainy Bigfoot video that looks suspiciously like me walking down my driveway to bring the garbage out.

And my feet, liberated after doing time in the witness protection program, require far more work than an ordinary pedicure. Instead, I get on Angie's List to locate a general contractor who can bring in a backhoe and asphalt grader before wearing sandals.

My swimsuit from the year before never fits or is horrible in some way that I only realize after looking at pictures of myself having spent the previous summer in it. So, I'm tasked with finding a new one. Defying all laws of physics, it's required to cover all my problem areas without leaving just a patch of my forehead visible. This is usually unattainable.

The good news is that I don't need sunscreen. For some inexplicable reason, I can't seem to stop buying it as if I'm planning to relocate to the equator. There's a rubber crate full in the garage, more in my beach bags, and I'm considering an underground bunker in case we're approaching end of days.

It's probably because I grew up in the '80s when catastrophic sunburns were not just acceptable, but encouraged. Back then we didn't sweat the small stuff like melanoma and skin damage. Instead we lathered up with baby oil, squeezed lemon juice in our hair, and made laying out a full-time career.

On the first 67-degree day in the spring of 1983, I dutifully put on my swimsuit, grabbed a spray bottle, and headed out the backyard for my inaugural summer burn. My dad, a photographer, had a large reflector crafted from aluminum foil, which I borrowed to maximize my time in the sun.

In a lawn chair, holding up what loosely resembled a piece of the space shuttle, and listening to Toto lament how losing Rosanna could hurt so bad, I sat for nearly five hours.

I couldn't have been more scorched if I'd been handed down a guilty verdict by the Salem witch jury.

Giant flakes of skin peeled off my face and body for weeks after and I endured the stares of my high school classmates who couldn't decide if I had bathed in boric acid or was just molting.

Things are a lot different now, of course. Kids aren't even allowed outside anymore unless they're wearing hazmat suits and SPF's of 100^2. Even my husband is afraid of the sun and fears getting sunburned more than carjacked.

Because of this, when we go to the beach, he spends at least an hour meticulously spackling on lotion thicker than drywall cement and then performs the unholy miracle of coming home a shade lighter than when he left.

My teenagers, however, seem doomed to repeat history. Last year on a trip to Florida, my oldest daughter blatantly disregarded my warnings and pleadings to sunscreen her sickly, New England skin.

After five hours of lying on her stomach, she was transformed into the human version of a Monte Cristo sandwich; cheese on one side and ham on the other. Every time she sat, stood, walked, inhaled, or blinked, she was acutely reminded of her unfortunate decision.

And when her skin began peeling off in giant flakes, I asked her if she'd bathed in boric acid or was just molting.

I guess things aren't so different after all.

Bad Passenger

As sea of red brake lights glow in front of me, I slam down on mine in anticipation of a quick stop. From behind the steering wheel my husband shoots me a tired look and asks, "How's that invisible passenger brake working out for you over there?"

"Not very well," I reply. "Maybe we should get it looked at."

I'm aware that in terms of riding shotgun, I'm about as fun as sharing toenail clippers at a fungus convention. But it's not my fault. I suffer from Episodic Automobile Freak-Out Disorder, or EAFOD [pronounced eee-**faw**-d] as it's more commonly known.

Though largely ignored by the medical community, EAFOD is a rare, but serious condition, where afflicted persons frequently suffer from wide-eyed, facial flinching, profuse sweating, uncontrollable spasms of the arms and legs, involuntary verbal outbursts like "*WatchoutWatchoutWatchout*," along with the indiscriminate use of four-letter words, compulsive side mirror checking, all which occur while traveling as a passenger in a car.

It's incurable.

Initial onset occurred in my early adulthood after spending a significant amount of time in the car with my brother, David.

No ride with Dave was ever complete without at least one near-death experience. An Honors graduate from the Lindsay Lohan School of Driving, he had the uncanny ability to sift through his entire CD collection while changing lanes at eighty miles an hour.

Also, an attentive conversationalist, he liked to make prolonged, steady eye contact with me as I sat, rigid with apprehension, in the passenger seat. I rarely returned the favor as I was too preoccupied with looking forward and pointing out roadside attractions like stoplights and pedestrians.

When riding together, I habitually found myself saying his

name in some combination of inquiry and terror. "Dave? Dave? Dave? Dave! *Dave*! *Dave*! DAVE!" Then, after a swerve and catastrophic near miss, he'd calmly look over at me and say, "What?"

Now, years later, my brother still becomes irritated if I mention his driving and the words "primal fear" in the same sentence and then pointedly reminds me of the time that, itching to use my newly minted driver's license, I insisted on driving him to the mall.

At cruising speed, I hit a large pool of standing water in the middle of the road and lost control of the car. Like a scene from "The Matrix," we stared at one another in slow motion as the car did a series of whooshing, 360 spins before eventually coming to a stop beneath a billboard that read, "Jesus Loves You."

It would be years before Dave agreed to ride with me again.

In addition to my passenger disability, I also suffer from EAFOD's sister affliction, Episodic *Airplane* Freak-Out Disorder. It's a relatively mild case considering there are only a few things that really bother me about flying, including check-in, boarding, ascending, descending, and every moment in between.

The good news is that I've found a treatment that helps manage my symptoms.

It's a remedy that I like to call "Xan Grigio," which consists of a single Xanax washed down with a liberal amount of white wine. My prescription bottle specifically warns against this because it can apparently cause drowsiness, difficulty concentrating, and impair thinking.

Well, *duh*.

If I actually wanted to think about flying 32,000 feet above the earth in a soup can, I wouldn't need Xan Grigio in the first place. Impairment is not a side effect, it's the objective. Without it, the flight attendants would have to pry me off the exit door, where I'd be clinging like one of those suction-cup Garfield dolls you see in the back of car windows.

Of course, you should never try this at home and certainly don't cite me if you do. Equally, if my doctor is reading this, I just made up all that stuff about Xanax and wine. Wait, what?

As for my brother, he lives abroad and will probably never read this. If he does, however, I want to state for the record that he is the best, safest driver on the road, no matter what country he's in; just as long as it's not this one.

Shopping Personality Test

I'VE DISCOVERED THAT WHEN IT COMES TO SHOPPING, MOST people fall into a handful of easily distinguishable categories. In order to identify the various types, I've compiled this helpful guide.

The Power Shopper
With a strategy and itemized list in hand, Power Shoppers cannot be bothered with the menial task of searching for gifts. No, the Power Shopper is simply too busy with work, kids, sports, or other pressing demands like watching the season finale of "The Bachelor," to devote more than a single day, mapped out to the minute, in order to get the job done.

Methodically working their way through various big box stores, they nab the first thing that marginally meets their criteria before crossing it off the list and immediately moving on to the next item. Pajama pants for Kaye? Check. A leaf blower for Bob? Yep. Gift card for the coach? Done.

As the sun sets, the Power Shopper, sweaty from exertion, heads out to the car with bags in one hand and energy bar in the other, satisfied by another mission accomplished and with enough time leftover to hit the gym on the way home.

The Onliner
With little patience for the mall and even less for other people, the Onliner bypasses the whole leaving-the-house thing, preferring to make purchases from the relative safety of their computer monitor.

Fortified with an Amazon Prime account and holed up at a corner desk, they suffer from acute red-eye fatigue and finger cramps after hours of intense clicking for just the right friendship necklace. They celebrate Cyber Monday like a national holiday and occasionally forsake getting dressed or brushing their teeth in lieu of locating a fifty-inch, flat screen for less than a hundred bucks.

With a fortress of boxes piled on their front step, they maintain a love-hate relationship with the UPS guy who doesn't appreciate delivering forty-pound bags of cat litter or daily Zappos boxes (free shipping included!) but who will likely retire independently wealthy from the Onliner's purchases alone.

The Treasure Hunter

The most attentive and thoughtful of all shoppers, the Treasure Hunter spends weeks, sometimes months picking out just the right thing for you, guaranteeing that you'll feel like a complete heel for the impersonal candle you threw into a used gift bag before leaving the house.

It's not uncommon for Treasure Hunters to keep a three-ring binder on hand to store the perfect greeting card they bought for you last March. And they are always prepared with spare, just-in-case gifts from everyone's favorite stores for any last-minute holiday gathering or get together.

With coordinating paper and bows, their flawlessly wrapped presents often inspire recipients to exclaim, "Oh, this looks so nice that I don't even want to open it!" And subsequently making everyone else's gifts appear as though they were fished straight out of a dumpster.

The Re-Gifter

When most of us receive a sweater or some other item we're not crazy about, we typically return or exchange it. The Re-Gifter, however, stores unwanted gifts as inventory and keeps them on hand for the next time they're required to produce one for any variety of occasions.

Regardless of whether or not their fifteen-year-old niece wants an electric deep fryer for her birthday, the Re-Gifter will carefully package it up with recycled paper saved from other gifts and give it anyway. It's not the thought that counts, but rather the gift.

When stock runs low, it's not uncommon for Re-Gifters to pillage their own personal items for presents and recipients shouldn't be surprised to receive "heirloom" jewelry, a shirt that-I-only-wore-once, or a nice bottle of wine that someone else brought to the party.

The Biodegrader

Gifts from the socially-conscious Biodegrader never include animal by-products, GMO's or unrecycled plastic. Wrapped in paper made from sustainable forests, Biodegraders want to help make the world a better place through each and every purchase. And they never forget their reusable bags in the car.

Typical gifts from the Biodegrader include things you can't actually use like a star named after your firstborn or lifelong financial support for a colony of Chilean alpacas. Rounding out the list are tie-dye hoodies, multi-vitamin packs and anything made from hemp.

They are also not afraid to gift home-baked goods like gluten-free quinoa balls or cookies made from flax seed and agave. And if they are bringing a holiday dish to share, you can be sure it'll come served with arrowroot gravy.

The Impulse Buyer

An economy-sized pack of Big Red? A set of Eiffel Tower drinking cups? You never know what the Impulse Buyer will purchase next, but you can be sure that it wasn't planned or well-thought-out. This shopper is the sole reason that there are trial-size bottles of Febreeze and corn nuts in the checkout lane.

Armed and dangerous with a MasterCard, Impulse Buyers will throw just about anything into their carts and it's not out of the question to receive lavender hand soaps one year and a protractor the next.

With their heads on a swivel, Impulse Buyers are easily

identifiable in stores looking back and forth to ensure they haven't missed anything they might want to buy and usually obstruct the checkout aisle debating whether or not to throw in Scotty dog-shaped shortbread cookies at the last minute.

The Laser Striker

The Laser Striker is typically male and, much like the Death Star, the Laser Striker zeros in on the one thing they need and will not be deterred from going in after it as part of a dedicated military operation.

The force is strong with these shoppers and even a fresh rack of football jerseys or aviator sunglasses will not distract them from their single-focused determination to get in, purchase athletic socks, and escape without detection.

Threatening the entire mission, however, is the unexpected tagalong wife or girlfriend, who will insist on stopping and looking at every single item from one corner of the store to the other (usually more than once) thus rendering the strike completely ineffective thus requiring a new, covert plan of attack be drawn up as soon as possible.

The Bargain Binger

Finally, it doesn't matter if it's a broken bike lock or a one-armed turtleneck, the Bargain Binger sees a red "Clearance" sticker and like runway lights on an airfield, comes in for a landing.

In order of importance, the relevance of a gift often comes in a distant third after sale price and availability. Receivers shouldn't be surprised if they find a porcelain dolphin figurine or blinding neon sweater hidden beneath the tissue paper. The tag is carefully cut to suggest the Bargain Binger paid full price for your personal grooming kit, but everyone knows better and no one should expect a gift receipt.

Upon checking out, the Bargain Binger rarely owes any money as they often have enough promotional coupons stuffed in their wallet to have earned cash back or at the very least some kind of store credit.

Snowpocalypse Now

Most days I enjoy going to the grocery store about as much as I like scooping the litter box. With both I'm required to use cheap, plastic bags that allow everything to dump out of the bottom, and whatever I end up picking out is almost always something I don't want.

That probably explains why general panic sets in when I see the forecast calling for more than three inches of snow. It means that I am obligated to hit the grocery store in anticipation of what I like to call New England Armageddon.

I've never understood why potential snow accumulation requires everyone to flock to the store in sweaty alarm to stock up on eggs, milk and bread. Because while I like French toast as much as the next person, I'm pretty sure that I can get through a day or two without it if necessary.

In spite of that, I still find myself swept up in the snowpocalypse hysteria. Even if I just cleaned off the shelves of a warehouse club the day before, I rush off to the store just in case I missed something I just can't live without for three or four hours till the snowplow comes through.

Once I get there, I usually end up buying a bunch of weird stuff that I don't actually need like thumb tacks and oat bran in the event that I decide to redecorate and correct any occasional irregularities at the same time.

What always surprises me is why there isn't a line of cars blocking the entrance to the local package store. Because, let's be honest, if it came down to being trapped in the house with my husband or kids for some indefinite length of time and I had to choose between food and merlot, I'm sure I could stand to lose a few pounds.

You think I'd be used to bad weather. I grew up in Minnesota where snow is more abundant than oxygen and the only two seasons are winter and Mother's Day. Because of that, nothing short of a direct comet strike shuts down the state. Subsequently, there weren't too many snow days when I was a kid, at least not at my school, where "Snow or Die" was the motto.

It didn't matter if every city block within a 400-mile radius was destroyed in some sort of artic tsunami, Kennedy Elementary School remained open. And thanks to my parents who didn't want my brother and me in the house any longer than required, if there was a school bus anywhere nearby, we were on it, regardless of whether it came after lunch or if it was sticking out of a ditch.

One year, after an unfortunate series of events left us with a record amount of snow and a broken snow blower, my dad freaked out and insisted that we clear our long, gravel driveway without the benefit of any sort of heavy equipment, so he could go to work.

Because there were only two shovels and my dad suffered from a "bad back," my mom and I were recruited for active duty.

For hours we worked while he stood with his hands on his hips and supervised our progress. As we finally closed in on the end of the driveway, my shovel broke in half from the weight of the snow. Relieved, I assumed that this meant that my tenure as a human backhoe was over.

Instead, I watched as my dad disappeared into the garage for a few minutes before returning and handing me a dustpan.

Eventually we finished the job and my dad was liberated. Frankly, we weren't sorry to see him go.

Sometimes I like to think about what my kids would say if I told them they had to go out and shovel our driveway with a couple of dust pans. Lucky for them, we have a guy who plows making that scenario unlikely to play out in real life.

And now that I think about it, going to the grocery store and scooping the litter box don't seem so bad.

I'm Gonna

IF CHANGING NAMES WAS EASY, I'D HAVE DITCHED THE WHOLE "Sarah" thing by elementary school and gone with "Elizabeth," the one I wish my parents had chosen instead.

Unlike my name, which had no fun abbreviations and was only shortened to "Sar" when my mom was mad, Elizabeth could be modified into other, more interesting variations like Liz, Lizzy, and Beth (my favorite Kiss song).

Wesley, my last name, might have been cool if kids had nicknamed me "Wes," like my brother.

Instead, some junior rocket scientist came up with "Wesson-Oil," a considerably less flattering epithet, but one that stuck right up until I graduated.

By high school, my wish-name was "Tatiana," or "Tat" for short.

I chose it after reading a Harlequin Romance where the heroine learns her billionaire boss, Julian Thorn, has been cold and aloof because he fell in love with her the moment she showed up on his doorstep, penniless and suffering from amnesia.

Afraid of love, Julian confesses to Tatiana in the last paragraph of the last page, that it made him angry to love her, he didn't want to love her, but, dammit, he loves her so much it hurts.

I seriously contemplated going legal with it until I shared it with a classmate, who snickered and pointed out that just adding a "w" to "Tat" gave my catchy new nickname an entirely different spin, effectively putting an end to that phase.

When it comes to changing monikers, a friend of mine insists that instead of using her first name I should call her, "I'm Gonna" after all the things she plans to accomplish, but never manages to.

I understand.

There are a lot of things I'm gonna do, too.

Each morning, I'm gonna pour myself into some Lycra and run a half marathon before my second cup coffee.

Then I'm gonna spend the rest of the day either fasting or at the very least, avoiding all carbs, refined sugar, and the Wendy's drive thru.

After I finish the laundry, I'm gonna do the Marshalls return that's been sitting in the back of my car, thirty days past the purchase date. Sorry, store credit only.

I'm also gonna read all the self-help books I've had rush-shipped on Amazon Prime, then I'm gonna clean the bathroom, a hair garden and mold hotel all in one.

While I'm at it, I'm gonna clean out my drawers in an effort to finally get rid of all the clothes that don't fit, likely leaving a handful of stretched-out Jockey underpants and a pair of flannel pajama bottoms when I'm done.

When I have a few extra hours to spend on hold, I'm gonna call my cell phone provider to speak to someone about the mysterious international charge billed to my account, before being transferred to someone else, who will transfer me to someone else, who just might be able to help credit the $3.18 I have coming.

And, one day, I'm gonna use the photo scanner I bought to scan the 7,000 assorted pictures shoved into a Rubbermaid up in the attic, which I'm gonna organize instead of parking it on the couch to watch another episode of *House Hunters International*.

If nothing else, "I'm Gonna" is better than the alternative, "I Probably Shouldn't, But…"

This alias precedes most, if not all bad decisions like "I probably shouldn't, but I'm going to open another bottle of wine anyway," or "I probably shouldn't, but it's by the side of the road and free!"

"I Probably Shouldn't, But…" also applies to anytime I take a credit card out of my wallet or leave it in arm's reach of the computer.

This can be particularly dangerous if I'm buying shoes or

looking up airfares to Europe, since I have no business doing either.

And definitely not after "I probably shouldn't, but I'm going to open another bottle of wine anyway."

It's safe to assume no one will ever suggest that I change my name to "I Don't Really Need It," except maybe the people who give me lotion samples at the mall. And my husband.

Otherwise, I doubt I've ever even said those words, let alone used them while looking over a dessert menu.

All things considered I think I'll stick with "Sarah." Unless, of course, Mrs. Julian Thorn is still available.

Buddy and the Urinator

MOST PEOPLE LIKE EITHER DOGS OR CATS. I'M A CAT PERSON.

That's probably because when I was growing up, our dog, Max, an amicable cockapoo, routinely gobbled feminine products out of the garbage and used the braided rug in our living room as a city park.

At least once a week I'd come running in, barefoot, to watch Half-Pint give Nellie Oleson a piece of her mind on TV, before feeling the unmistakable squish between my toes and gagging off to the bathroom.

Max was also a barker. He barked at the mailman, the neighbors, the septic tank. It was like he was rehearsing to cut one of those doggie Christmas albums in a single take, including "Jingle Bells" and "Good King Wenceslas."

It's no wonder that as an adult, I prefer the quiet, non-tampon eating, poop-in-a-box, sort of pet.

When our kids were little, we adopted Spooky, a sweet cat, whose only fault was frequent hairballs. One time she vomited directly into my open jewelry box, requiring a massive, Exxon-Valdez, cleanup effort if I ever planned on wearing my earrings again.

To keep Spooky company, we added Daisy, a stray kitten. A few years later came Buddy, a rescue cat, in a need of a home.

First of all, anyone who says that there's no difference between owning two cats or three is lying.

Effective immediately, our relatively peaceful home was transformed into a 24-hour animal shelter, with multiple litter boxes, bowls of stinky food pebbles, and hissing cats everywhere.

The new couches we'd saved years for were repurposed into walnut-beige scratching posts, something I can only assume Pottery Barn didn't take into account when they upholstered them with delicate, special order, linen.

And no one left the house without looking like they'd first pulled their coat out of a barbershop trash can.

The bigger problem, however, was that Buddy and Daisy didn't seem to get along.

My first clue was discovering that over the course of a couple months, they had systematically peed on every rug, in every single room of our house.

For good measure, they also hit a few bookshelves, the front door, coffee table, shower curtain, bath towels, most radiators, and a laundry basket full of my favorite clothes in some epic, feline territory war.

Though I knew something smelled off, my husband insisted that it was just his coffee, leading me to wonder if he was spooning in ammonia instead of Splenda, which, at least, would explain why he couldn't tell the difference.

It's been seven years since The War of the Cats began. Spooky has since retired to the great litterbox in the sky, leaving Buddy and Daisy behind to continue their festering urine feud.

As a result, we've divided our house into two, separate, cat zones to ensure that we don't have to burn it down when we move out.

The upstairs belongs to Daisy, the more frequent urinator, and the downstairs, Buddy.

Since cats don't really respect invisible boundaries, we've been forced to employ drastic measures to make it work.

Hours of searching the internet produced the Scat Mat solution. It apparently teaches your pet to "avoid areas that you want to protect," by using a "gentle," static impulse.

Though the cats have been largely unfazed by the introduction of electroshock therapy, the rest of us have stepped on it enough times to be terrified of going upstairs for anything other than an obvious emergency.

Because the mat wasn't effective, we also set up a tall iron gate, creating an East-West Berlin situation in the middle of our hallway.

Simple things like doing laundry require strategizing,

considering that the washer is located across the border.

And guests who want to come upstairs must first pass through Checkpoint Charlie, displaying proper credentials and agreeing not to pee in any of the bedrooms before being allowed in.

Even so, the cats still fight through the slats of the gate.

Short of installing a drawbridge and moat, there's not much else we can do besides wait it out.

Once they've used up what's left of their nine lives, it's unlikely that I will ever be convinced to get replacements, because come to think of it, I'm not a cat person after all.

The Toe Incident

By all accounts, I've been pretty lucky when it comes to injuries and medical issues.

I've only had two official-ish surgeries (anything removed by tweezers in the bathroom notwithstanding) and both of them were dental.

Oh sure, I've had my share of mishaps. A couple rounds of stitches when I was a kid, countless flights over my bike handlebars into the pavement, some Band-Aid-worthy hangnails.

One time, after doing yard work, I wheelbarrowed the debris into the woods, trapesing through a patch of shiny, three-leafed plants along the way.

This resulted in an industrial-grade case of poison ivy severe enough to require the widespread use of gauze, scare small children, and prompt a Code Red at the World Leprosy Organization.

But otherwise, no broken arms, splenectomies or anything noteworthy outside of the toe incident.

Most everyone has broken at least one, if not more, of their toes doing something uneventful like cutting it too close to the bed, or grossly misjudging the distance between their foot and the doorjamb.

It's a governing law of physics, much like the one that decrees that any time you're experiencing a sweaty, gastrointestinal emergency, the closest toilet is 400 miles away, or located in a public square.

And everyone has a Toe Tale to tell.

My husband once broke his toe after rolling my hundred-pound suitcase over it on our way to the airport. A friend snapped her longer-than-average middle toe walking up cement steps in a pair of flipflops.

Though technically not a fracture, my dad sheared off the

nail on his big toe pulling the vacuum cleaner back from a forward pass with a little too much force. And one of my kids took out a toe going to the bathroom in the middle of the night.

In the summer of 2004, we were selling our first house. In anticipation of strangers touring our home like a Disney park, we were feverishly cleaning out closets, cupboards, and every other space to make it appear as though we lived like ordinary people instead of livestock.

It was while most everything we owned was haphazardly strewn on every inch of free real estate in the house, that our very orderly neighbor called to let us know that he was stopping by.

Having easily gone two days without showering, wearing half clothes, half pajamas, I panicked and began running around in a futile attempt at damage control.

Directly between the kitchen and dining room is where my little toe caught on the edge of our oak microwave cabinet.

Sounding similar to a base hit at a Red Sox game, the pain was white hot and immediate.

Shrieking and writhing on the floor, my husband rushed in with a litany of "Oh my Gods," and immediately began preparing to go to the emergency room.

With our kids too young to stay home alone, I called my mom with a frantic SOS, and begged her to come.

Mildly put out by my drama, she asked why I couldn't just tape it.

Under most circumstances, a reasonable solution.

Unless I ever planned on wearing shoes again.

Which would require all my toes facing in the same general direction.

Instead, I'd somehow managed to break it in a way that left my little piggy sticking out the side of my foot like a backwards anvil. And without some kind of medical intervention, it was never going to cry wee-wee all the way home, again.

Ever.

My mom came, reluctantly, and we left for the urgent care clinic.

Upon arriving, the check-in nurse smiled pleasantly and asked the reason for my visit.

Before I could answer, her eyes traveled downward, settling on my right foot.

"Ohhhhh," she said. "Never mind."

Once in a room, there were X-Rays and a stream of medical personnel, parading in and out, all gawking at my backwards side-toe.

A grim-faced nurse laid out that I was likely staring down the barrel of serious baby toe surgery if I ever hoped to use it again.

In the end, she just stuck a needle full of Novocain into my foot, and the doctor carefully picked up my toe, turned it right-side, then forward, before taping it to its big brother and sending me home with crutches.

A few weeks later our house sold, and we moved. The microwave cabinet, however, stayed behind.

The Cargument

As a kid I was fortunate enough to tag along with my grandparents on a number of road trips.

From the Rocky Mountains to Yellowstone National Park, I viewed some of the Midwest's finest attractions from the back-seat of their used, blue Cadillac.

Shortly after merging onto the interstate, my grandmother would reach into her purse and pull out rosary beads. Together we'd recite an hour's worth of Our Fathers, along with a hand-ful of other prayers about virgins, ghosts, and abject suffering thrown in for good measure.

Depending on where we were headed, she'd sometimes wrap it up with the Stations of the Cross, ensuring that we were up to date on our devotions just in case God planned to kill us off before we reached Mount Rushmore.

In retrospect, I'm fairly certain that she also prayed because after years of riding shotgun with my grandfather, she recognized that divine intervention was the only thing standing between them and a hearing in divorce court.

It wasn't that he was a bad driver, they just didn't see eye-to-eye on some of the basics like navigation, direction, steering, passing, braking, and parking.

I can still remember my grandmother admonishing my grandfather for his lead foot, among other things.

In a clipped tone, she'd simply say, "speed," a couple of times, before becoming annoyed when he didn't actually slow down.

At that point she'd disapprovingly say his name, elongating each syllable to let him know she meant business.

"Eddy. Ed-deeeee!"

"What?" he'd finally bark at her.

"Watch your speed!"

And for a short time, he'd oblige.

Eventually, however, the lure of the gas petal proved to be too much, and the speedometer would creep back up, starting the whole thing over again.

The reason I bring this up is that while my husband and I seldom argue, when we do, it's almost always in the car.

While possible that it's a heredity thing, the more likely explanation is that, of the two of us, I clearly have a superior command of the road.

Even from the passenger seat.

Though I've repeatedly tried to make him aware of this, he still ignores my driving tips and the constructive criticism that I like to volunteer when he's behind the wheel.

In fact, sometimes it makes him mad.

Once, after politely requesting that he leave enough space to insert a slice of American cheese between our car and the one in front us, he blew up, for no apparent reason, and accused me of having a "stunning" lack of depth perception.

In that moment I could have retorted that when it comes to noticing stuff that needs to be done around the house, he suffers from the exact same disability.

But instead I chose to be the bigger person.

And, in glacial silence, I allowed him to reflect on his words for the remaining seven hours and forty-three minutes of our eight-hour road trip to Canada, and into the next day before finally receiving a begrudging apology.

Another time, after shrilly pointing out that his driving was providing me with a near-death experience (tunnel, lost relatives, white light and all) he angrily snapped that if I didn't like what I was seeing, I could shut my eyes.

Since at least one of us needed to watch the road, I felt like I should keep mine open in case he decided to make any further life-threatening decisions in an attempt to find a parking spot.

This particular exchange resulted in a nuclear winter lasting until we could both agree that he was wrong and would take any future driving "suggestions" under consideration without getting upset.

After all, I'm only trying to help.

Besides it's good for him to be reminded of a few things including a ride to The Home Depot for light bulbs shouldn't require a box of Dramamine, coordinates can be entered into the GPS before leaving the driveway, and although most highways have a left lane, we don't always need to be in it.

Also, the lure of the gas petal sometimes proves to be too much for him, so you'd think he'd be more appreciative of my vigilant monitoring of the speedometer, ensuring not only our safety, but that of everyone else on the road too.

Except he isn't.

At all.

Hopefully one day he'll realize the full extent of my benevolence.

Until then, there's always the rosary.

Happiest Place on Earth

MY DAD LIKES TO TALK ABOUT THE TIME WE TOOK A FAMILY vacation to Disneyland when my brother was thirteen, and I was eight.

After shelling out a small fortune for unlimited passes (not to mention roundtrip airline tickets to California), my parents dropped us off at the park then returned to our hotel to enjoy a day of not having to go to the park.

Hot and tired after merely an hour, my brother and I agreed that our time would be better spent swimming in the hotel pool and caught a shuttle bus back to the Travelodge.

Upon our unexpected return, we were greeted by a dark room and two hostile parents who blamed their disheveled appearance on being interrupted during what they claimed was a "mid-morning nap."

After the whole Bored-at-Disney thing, my dad swore he'd never take us anywhere again outside of the Sunset Inn, a motor lodge with an indoor swimming pool, located ten miles from our house.

I give him credit for making good on his promise.

From Hawaii to Italy, my parents went on to travel the world.

Alone.

Not that I blame them.

I have since traveled to Disney with my kids.

More than once.

It's like doing time in the clink, except not as fun and no one gets parole.

The first time we visited, our daughters were seven and five.

Aside from a complete family meltdown over what brand of orange juice the hotel restaurant served, record-breaking attendance during a record-breaking heatwave, and me being stricken with the flu, it was a good time.

I can still recall being in a fever dream with 37,000 other sweaty people, Kleenex stuffed up each nostril, praying for Tinkerbell to cue the fireworks so I could take the shuttle full of BO and crying children back to the hotel and die in peace.

Or, at the very least, in an air-conditioned room.

Blessed with two kids terrified by automatic flushing toilets, I recall crouching on the floor of every bathroom stall in Disney World, covering the sensor with my hand, because if it unexpectedly flushed while either one of them was using it, they'd shriek and run regardless of whether they'd finished or not.

By day's end, there was almost always a hysterical crying fit along with pleas to go home, to which my husband would respond by saying that we'd paid for the week and I would just have to stick it out.

I read somewhere that women are biologically programmed to forget the suffering and trauma associated with childbirth, so they'll be willing to reproduce more than once.

Under the same principle, I signed up for another Disney trip the following year.

With the Great Orange Juice Crisis resolved (but not toilet flushing), things were nominally better, apart from another health issue.

We were hemorrhaging money.

A princess breakfast cost more than the mortgage on our house, requiring emergency first aid from Visa just so I could watch my daughters hug Snow White and my husband pretend that he wasn't watching Jasmine.

And with glittery gift shops located at the end of each attraction, exiting Space Mountain without buying a snow globe was like negotiating a hostage release with miniature terrorists strung out on adrenaline and Mickey Mouse ice cream bars.

Then there were the spray fans.

Considering that Disney in May is hotter than camping on

the sun, the portable water misters for sale on every corner were nothing short of salvation.

But at $35 a pop, it came down to a choice between temporary relief from the heat, or food for the rest of the trip.

We bought the spray bottle.

This immediately prompted a hockey brawl between our kids, barely capable of sharing the same oxygen, let alone a single misting fan.

With the Great Spray Bottle Feud underway and no Xanax vending machine nearby, I purchased a second one, which ultimately proved to be the spray-bottle-that-broke-the-husband's-back.

Soon he and I were also engaged in a full-blown domestic dispute, complete with finger pointing on whose fault it was for having raised children who couldn't appreciate the extreme sacrifices their parents made just to provide them with the opportunity to throw up on the Dumbo ride.

Fortunately, we managed to patch things up before the Main Street Electrical Parade, and shortly after we returned home, we planned our next vacation.

It was to the motor lodge, located ten miles from our house.

The Goldilocks Swimsuit

M<small>Y</small> <small>FAVORITE SWIMSUIT IS A RED ONE-PIECE, COVERED IN</small> flowers.

The last time I had it on, I was seven.

Which, coincidentally, is also the last time I remember wearing next to nothing in public and feeling pretty good about it. Except for the time I had too many glasses of wine at a Pampered Chef party.

Beyond that, however, I've never owned a single bathing suit that I hoisted on, and immediately thought, "Yes, this is IT! I found it!"

The perfect, covering-the-parts-I-want-to-hide garment to be worn in front of strangers, friends, loved ones, as well as photographed in from unflattering angles-I-didn't-even-know-I-had, suit.

It's not from lack of trying.

Finding one that fits my body type has proven elusive.

Because while retailers advertise swimsuits for every conceivable shape and size, including busty, slim, tall, short, lean, apple, pear, triangle, and the one person who can wear Victoria's Secret, I have yet to find a suit specifically designed for the ravioli figure; even though that's exactly the method I used to achieve it.

Operating under the Grenades and Horseshoes Principle, I've purchased a variety styles over the years, attempting to come close.

Unfortunately, outside of being really into Seal in the early 2000's, I share nothing in common with Heidi Klum, let alone the supermodel DNA necessary for me to feel comfortable prancing around a pool in a skin-tight leotard.

Although, for the sake of full disclosure, I did buy a snakeskin swimsuit in Mexico once while on college spring break.

Under the influence of unlimited tanning sessions and tequila shooters, it seemed like a good idea, even if it did have a plunging neckline and bold cutouts in all the places it shouldn't have.

For an entire week, I paraded around in the suit at the beach. The bar. The hotel pool.

Taking pictures and flaunting regions best left hidden, I got my sexy on.

Until I sobered up and returned stateside.

It's for this reason, alone, I'm thankful that instead of Facebook, we just had the local Fotomat back then, and aside from the photo technician, the only evidence of the suit remains packed away in my attic, and not on the internet.

Outside of the Cancun incident, I've spent the majority of my life pursuing the Goldilocks swimsuit, and subsequently worn just about every kind.

The floral one-piece with accompanying "fun and flirty," wraparound scarf, which turns out to be neither since I can't figure out how to tie it properly without looking like Mrs. Howell from *Gilligan's Island*.

The "tankini," a suit whose sole purpose is to make trips to the bathroom easier than attempting to molt out of a wet, one-piece during four-alarm bladder crisis.

And while it's nice in theory, the tankini provides zero tailgate coverage, rendering it useless for my specific needs.

Pairing the tankini with board shorts (required for all the surfing I do) was my default option for a long time, until browsing through some vacation photos, I realized that the combination made me appear as though I was preparing to compete in the state high school wrestling tournament, minus the headgear.

I went shopping the next day.

Post-tankini came the Skirt Phase.

The skirt felt like a reasonable compromise. Carefree, but sensible. A little saucy, a little skin, but without giving away the farm.

For every suit, there was a skirt.

Short, flouncy, fitted, frilly; I had them all, and pleated polyester was my friend.

Eventually, the friendship waned when the Olympic-Ice-Dancer-On-The-Beach look I was going for, fell out of favor, leaving me with few, if any, options.

Most recently, I purchased one of the new "Miracle" swim-suits, as they're called.

Which, if we're being honest right now, is kind of offensive given the implication that divine intervention is the only thing capable of making me look good without clothes on.

Regardless of how accurate it is.

Equipped with Lycra panels strong enough to tow an air-plane, my 'miracle' suit crushes, squeezes, and sculpts my body beyond recognition; obviously the objective.

However, by design, it's nearly impossible to put on or remove without cutting off circulation to most of my extremities and requires medical intervention every time I wear it.

It's the closest thing to perfect I've found yet.

Words with Ex-Friends

I'M NOT REALLY INTO GAMES.

Other than losing at Battleship and attempting a few rounds of Guitar Hero, where I imagine I'm Eddie Van Halen but appear as though I'm having a seizure, I largely avoid them.

Growing up, my brother and I would pass boring Midwest days by eating my dad's hidden stash of chocolate cookies and playing Monopoly.

Not content to use the chump change provided by the Parker Brothers, we'd fleece the cash from Hasbro's Game of Life and broker serious, high-stakes real estate deals.

Armed with corporate money, we'd negotiate over investment capital, zoning permits, and landing on Free Parking meant you could retire at fifty with a condo in Sarasota.

Since then, however, I've found better ways of using my free time like viewing animal friends' videos and examining unwanted hair on my chin.

I do, however, play Words with Friends on my phone.

Not a lot.

Only when I have a couple extra minutes before getting out of bed in the morning.

Or before going to bed at night.

Also, during work hours, afternoons, evenings, meals, family gatherings, vacations, and all other times that I'm not sleeping or in the shower.

I've played almost everyone who's willing to join me in the electrifying quest for triple letters and words that end in "Z."

But not always with the best results.

After playing against a friend for a few months, I became increasingly frustrated when I not only lost every single game but was defeated by a landslide.

My mounting feelings of inadequacy finally spurred me to

message her, and ask if she was cheating, prompting her swift resignation.

After what felt like a reasonable "cooling off" period, I invited her to a rematch.

And was declined.

Later I asked her about it over lunch, and she professed to have never received the request.

Something we both knew wasn't true and officially ending our Words with Friends relationship for the rest of all time.

I still see her name on my WWF "scoreboard," and she continues racking up more points than I could ever hope to.

Just not with me.

Another friend and I have been playing for years, and most of the time I lose to her too.

I'm not surprised. She's smarter than I am, and a vegetarian.

What does surprise me is that despite her superior skill at online word games, she's never sent me a single, legible text message.

Liberally using a combination of letters, numbers, and special characters, it's like trying to crack a secret, war-time telegram just to figure out what time we're meeting for dinner.

Wat u M fr &7 ltr. we gon 4 day, u?

Sometimes I hand the phone over to my daughters, hoping that because they are millennials, they're capable of transcribing her text version of Sanskrit.

Usually one of them can.

It's probably because she sends nearly 8,000 text messages a month, according to my Verizon bill, making her a veritable expert in the field.

I shouldn't complain about unintelligible messages since I often write myself reminders on a legal pad in our kitchen, only to return later and discover that I can't read my own handwriting.

This happened last winter when I saw the word "deicer" scribbled down and had no clue what it meant.

Days went by, and I burned more than a few brain cycles trying to decode my own message, but I couldn't decipher "deicer."

Finally, after a couple of weeks, the millennial texter came home from college and, in a last-ditch effort, I asked her if she could make sense of it.

"Sure," she said, after a quick glance.

"It says, 'de-icer.'"

After a snowstorm, our driveway had become a virtual skating rink. To minimize the risk of putting the postman in traction just to deliver the desk calendar I'd ordered on Amazon, someone had to pick up ice-melting pellets at the hardware store.

Mystery solved.

Though our Monopoly days are long behind us, my brother and I play an ongoing game of Words with Friends, which helps us stay connected even though we are on different continents.

In spite of an IQ assessment, which identified him as a genius when he was a kid (I forgive my parents for not bothering to put me through the same test), he's only beaten me twice in six years.

Which says something.

I'm just not sure what.

Company Clean

I RECENTLY READ SOMEWHERE THAT THE AVERAGE HOME SHOULD be deep cleaned twice a month, with things like floors and bathrooms getting a weekly wash.

Once I stopped laughing, it occurred to me that some people might actually clean that often and immediately grew concerned that my Only-If-The-Health-Department-Is-Coming regimen might be inadequate.

It's not that I don't clean.

I'll open mail and, like, load the dishwasher. The rest of it, however, feels a lot like housework, which I generally avoid.

Not because I'm not lazy or anything. I just don't see the value.

Shortly after vacuuming the kitchen, someone eats an entire bag of pita chips without bothering to use a plate and it's like the whole thing never happened.

I wash clothes and later find them being used as ad hoc carpeting in someone's bedroom.

I scrub the toilet and within a day or two some desperate family member pleads that they just can't wait any longer to use it.

At one point, I mentioned the futility and my disdain of housework to a therapist friend who helped rationalize it by asking if I minded doing other repetitive-but-necessary chores, like getting a haircut, trimming my nails or brushing my teeth.

Once she put it all into perspective, I realized that I do, in fact, mind every single one of those things, along with any other task that doesn't involve shopping or eating, and subsequently felt much better about it.

When I do clean, it's usually because we have company coming over, leaving me no choice but to make it appear as though it's safe to enter our house without a tetanus shot.

Typically, the amount of cleaning required depends solely on who the guests are, creating a cleaning rating system.

Hoping to gain a better understanding of the potential work and stress involved, my husband usually asks for the classification well in advance.

Though unspoken, he's really hoping to gauge the degree of irrational behavior he can expect from me, including shrill accusations over him not being NEARLY helpful enough, despite my repeated reassurances that I don't need help.

He also wants to assess how much money I'm liable to shell out on new placemats and votive candles in order to feel good about it all.

For the most part, cleaning falls into three, distinct categories.

Close friends, in for the long haul despite knowing all our flaws, as well as family members obligated by DNA, typically warrant the Cursory Clean.

This involves taking out the trash, closing doors to messy rooms, spraying Febreze, and giving the toilet a once-over with a disinfectant wipe.

If I happen to notice that there's more food under the kitchen cabinets than in the refrigerator, then I'll sweep only that area before calling it quits.

Group gatherings including holidays, birthdays, or neighbors require the Serious Clean.

More labor-intensive than the Cursory Clean, the Serious Clean can take up to several days and requires actual work, like washing stuff and running the self-clean cycle on the oven, followed by an immediate airing-out-of-the-house after acrid smoke pours out of it for three hours.

It's not uncommon for the Serious Clean to coincide with Attempting a New Recipe; a direct result of binging on the Food Network and overestimating my culinary skills.

It's a lethal combination and the outcome is almost always the same.

A mutant version of Coq au Vin or Baked Alaska, if prepared

in a cement mixer while blindfolded and using none of the correct ingredients.

Finally, there's the Company Clean, reserved for brand new guests and that one friend who organizes the water bottles in the fridge so all the labels face in the same direction.

Far from an ordinary clean, the Company Clean is nothing short of DEFCON 1.

Not only does everything in the house get scrubbed down and assessed for replacement, but undertaking a massive home renovation project isn't out of the question, like adding on a screened-in porch because we don't have an outdoor entertaining space.

In the end, it doesn't really matter, because inevitably I forget to do the one critical thing that only becomes apparent after it's too late.

Like the time we had guests over for a dinner party and one of them kicked off her sandals, only to step in cat vomit camouflaged by the rug under the dining room table.

On the upside, after that, the Coq au Vin didn't seem so bad.

The "Talent" Show

Outside of 4H meetings and sledding during recess, there wasn't a whole lot of action at my rural Minnesota elementary school, which explains why the annual spring talent show was such a big deal.

Far from a bunch of hacks banging out "Chopsticks" on the music teacher's piano, it was a high-stakes event, complete with American Idol-style auditions and dramatic cuts that left kids sobbing in the hallway.

No stranger to showbiz, I was an accomplished vocalist by the age of seven, having sung publicly in my grandparent's living room, the neighbor's backyard, and the brick ledge of our fireplace using the microphone from my Panasonic tape recorder.

I'd also done a handful of gigs at school. My brother, a sixth grader, would occasionally drop by my first-grade homeroom with his guitar, and together we'd perform a few of our favorite hits in front of the class.

Looking back, I can't help but wonder if anyone else thought it was a little weird that in the middle of arithmetic, my brother would knock on the door and like something out of "Hee Haw," we'd just break into song for no apparent reason.

Even if they did, they still let us do it, and we gained notoriety as Kennedy Elementary's very own Donny and Marie Osmond.

Unfortunately, my brother matriculated to junior high, leaving me behind, like Hall without Oats, a Tennille with no Captain, George Michael without nameless-dark-haired-guy-no-one-can-remember.

While it was rough, I taught myself how to play the ukulele and partnered with my best friend, Sandy, to audition for the talent show.

The obvious pick for a couple of second graders, we sang

"The Green, Green, Grass of Home," an old Elvis song about an inmate heading off to execution. Not only did we make the cut, we were the featured performers at the 1976 Spring Talent Show.

Riding on the coattails of our success, we began planning for the next year, but midway through third grade, Sandy dumped me for Amy, a fellow classmate, and I was forced to audition as a solo act.

Taking a cue from Marie, who'd coincidently struck out on her own after the "Donny and Marie Show," I sang "Paper Roses." Sandy, the traitor, auditioned with Roberta Flack's "Killing Me Softly." And Amy, her new best friend, jumped up and down on a mini-trampoline to a Monkees song.

When the finalists were announced, I, alone, emerged victorious.

Decked out in a "Little House on the Prairie" dress, I gave my best talent show performance to date, exacting revenge on Sandy and Amy, and cementing my reputation as a singing sensation.

By fourth grade, Sandy and I patched things up and tried out with Stephen Bishop's "On and On." I remember adding a few fancy, vocal trills, some grown-up vibrato, and an Eddie Van Halen-inspired ukulele solo in the middle for good measure.

When the list of performers came out, a girl dressed up like a Barbie Doll doing a robot dance made the cut, as did the gym teacher's daughter (nepotism, duh), playing a painful, off-pitch, recital piece on the flute.

We, however, did not.

With hot tears rolling down my face, I resolved that fifth grade would be THE year to remember.

Deciding to go solo once more, I searched to find just the right number, settling on a song by my favorite trio, Tony Orlando and Dawn. Though all these years later I still have no clue which of the two girls is actually "Dawn," and why the other one doesn't get a name. It seems pretty unfair when you think about it.

Anyway.

As I hoped, I made it into the show that year singing "Say, Has Anybody Seen My Sweet Gypsy Rose," a feel-good tune about a woman who ditches her family to become a stripper.

Wearing a too-big pantsuit borrowed from my mom and a flower tucked behind my ear, I belted out lyrics about Mary Jo dancing naked with rings on her fingers, bells on her toes, when, halfway through the song, the tie on my pants loosened.

In a life-imitates-art moment, they began to slide down.

At risk of performing my own burlesque show in front of 400 elementary kids, I frantically hitched them up and held them until the song was over.

The next day, when my class was asked what they liked best about the talent show, a kid I mostly hated raised his hand and responded, "The part where Sarah Wesley's pants fell down."

And just as I hoped, no one ever forgot.

You've Been Chopped!

WHEN IT COMES TO GUILTY PLEASURES, MINE INCLUDE LISTEN-
ing to Air Supply's "All Out of Love," consuming an entire
canister of Moose Munch popcorn in a single sitting, and
binge-watching *Chopped*. In a perfect world, it's some combination of all three, with bottle of Chardonnay nearby.

Chopped has long been a favorite of mine.

I love the moment when host Ted Allen dramatically lifts the
cover off the loser's dish and sighs, "Chef Blah Blah, you'vvveee
been chooopppppeeed," in a single, drawn-out, breath.

I also like the judges. Tough, but fair, Alex Guarnaschelli.
The overcooked pasta-hating Scott Conant. And saucy Aarón
Sánchez, who always pronounces Latino foods with a heavily
accented flair and roll of his tongue, making ingredients like
tortillas baked from minced grasshoppers sound like something
I might want to eat.

Sometimes I think I could be a contestant. I've had a lot of
experience. In fact, Food Network could swing by my house on
any given night and shoot an episode with little to no advance
warning.

Too lazy to hit the grocery store and almost always out of
food, I frequently cook dinner using only what I have on hand.
This usually includes some kind of freezer-burned meat, a can
of pumpkin expired in a different calendar year, and a pencil
sharpener.

Similar to the show, I often end up with a catastrophic injury,
like the time I invested in a porcelain paring knife. Sharper than
a French Revolution guillotine, the very first time I used it, I
sliced open a finger attempting to chop garlic.

Serious enough to require gauze and medical tape, I dressed
it, and returned to the task.

Apparently having learned nothing from the experience, I

immediately did it again, almost severing a finger off the good hand, leaving me with two heavily bandaged pointers and shutting down production for the rest of the night.

Like *Chopped*, the judges at my house are a tough crowd.

My husband; on a required low salt, low sugar diet. My eldest daughter; a vegetarian. And my youngest daughter; a medically diagnosed supertaster.

Supertasters, for the uninitiated, have exponentially more taste buds than ordinary people, making many foods too pungent, bitter, or sweet. In other words, it's statistically impossible to cook anything they will eat outside of plain pasta and frozen Eggo waffles.

Working under those conditions, the only thing I routinely put on the table that everyone agrees on is silverware.

Like most contestants, I have a compelling backstory. Growing up, my mom, who thankfully is still around and will hotly debate me on this, didn't like to cook.

Oh sure, she made us a lot of wonderful meals. But there were also plenty of nights where she'd take out all the pans and set them on the stove, indicating that at some point she planned on cooking something in them.

Instead they'd sit empty for a couple of hours before she'd default to Stouffer's Chicken Tetrazzini heated up in the microwave.

In similar fashion, she also liked to set the vacuum cleaner in middle of the room if we were expecting company, implying that they'd interrupted her just as she was preparing to go on a vacuum bender, even if it was the farthest thing from the truth.

When my mom did cook, everything was "gourmet."

If we ate our salad after dinner, it was because that's how the "gourmets" did it. If we used frozen orange juice in our Minute Rice, it was because that's how the "gourmets" ate it. If dessert consisted of a banana set into a pineapple ring, topped with Miracle Whip and a cherry, that was gourmet, too.

And because we lived twenty miles from the nearest grocery store, we rarely, if ever, had all the ingredients for any given recipe, which meant that nearly every meal included at least one inspired substitution.

An optimist, my mom believed that it was perfectly acceptable to swap one ingredient for another, as long as they both fell into the same general food group, especially when it came to dairy products.

Sour cream worked for whipped cream on top of gingerbread. Skim milk was a stand-in for Cool Whip, because who doesn't like that on top of sliced bananas? And since cottage cheese sounded a lot like ricotta cheese, they were virtually interchangeable.

When I think about it, my mom would have been the perfect contestant on *Chopped*. With all her gourmet dishes and creative improvising, she'd have won.

Spanx For Men

LIKE EVERYONE ELSE, I KEEP THE USUAL STUFF IN MY DRESSER. I have a drawer allocated for socks. A drawer for pajamas. I even have one for my "workout" clothes, an oxymoron since any kind of physical activity is the last thing I do in them.

There's also a drawer for my stash of undergarments. But not like bras and other lady stuff, I'm talking about shapewear.

If it slenderizes, smooths, secures, flattens, firms, tones, reduces, hides, pads, pushes up, pushes in, pushes out, condenses, conceals, controls or covers up anything flabby, saggy or loose, I own it.

I didn't always have such an extensive collection. In fact, prior to having kids and eating at the Olive Garden, I regularly left the house without wearing some form of restrictive Lycra under my clothes. But that was a long time ago.

Since then I've accumulated an impressive assortment of what lingerie companies like to call, "slimming intimates." Items specifically created to ensure that I look like every possible version of myself, except for the real one.

I'm hoping that the people who invented Space Saver Vacuum Seal Bags will come out with a similar product line for women. It's my dream to slip on a plastic bodysuit, attach it to my vacuum, then suck all the extra air out, instantly transforming me into a size two and conveniently allowing me to fit under the bed for extra storage.

I've decided that a lot of shapewear is named for scenarios that are never going to play out as long as you have it on.

Like, I'm pretty sure that the odds of any sort of "bliss" occurring while wearing the Blissful Benefits (No muffin Top) Hipster are about as good as getting shot with a hot, love arrow while wearing the Cupid Torsette with Extra Firm Tummy Control.

And, let's face it, "romping" is the one thing that's never going to happen with the Flexees Dreamwear, Wear-Your-Own-Bra, Romper, on.

Meanwhile, I can't help but wonder why women seem to be the only ones sinking huge sums of money into body altering underwear. After all, we aren't the only gender in need of some assistance.

Why aren't men's boxers made with a control top that helps to keep their tummy firm while hiding unsightly bulges?

Just where are the push-up, cotton briefs with underwire and extra padding to help them look one cup-size bigger? And I have yet to see a pair of swim trunks designed with "extra panels" to help flatter most any masculine figure.

But I guess you never know. Spanx, a brand of shapewear for women, recently unveiled a line of body shaping products for men.

They don't seem to be very popular though. Probably because, unlike women's, most men's styles have super boring names like the Cotton Control V-Neck or Comfort Trunk.

Maybe men would wear more shapewear if it sounded man-lier, like pickup trucks, which all seem to be named for the ferocity of their owner's, uh, horsepower. Like Ram, Titan, Super Duty and Big Horn.

If I was a guy with a problem waistline, I'd want to put on shapewear that controlled it with the strength of heavy machinery and the brute force of the NFL.

I'd totally be in for The Front Loader with Extra Lombardi Support or the Excavator with Gridiron Panels.

If my butt was saggy, I'd go for something that could get the job done with a serious dose of testosterone like the Backhoe, Dump Truck, or Heisman Forklift.

To hide unsightly panty lines beneath my Dockers I'd opt for the Hydraulic Log Splitter.

And for a little extra support with my man parts, I'd probably buy the Winner's Cup or the Toolbox.

It'll never happen though. Unlike women, men don't seem

motivated to shrink-wrap every inch of their body in the same material used to make surgical gloves just to go out to dinner.

Now that think about it, I should probably clean out my dresser. I could use the extra space for more important things, like clothes I actually want to wear.

Sick Flags

I've always loved rides. I was the kid who'd stand on tiptoes at the "You-Must-Be-This-Tall-to-Ride" sign, and then sob at the entrance when I didn't meet the height requirement for the roller coaster.

Almost all of my childhood birthdays were spent at Valleyfair, a wholesome, milk-drinking, Midwest amusement park not far from where I grew up.

The ritual was always the same. My mom would drop me and my friends off in the morning, returning later at an agreed upon time, to pick us up.

Most years, I'd conveniently "forget" when that was and hit each ride a few more times before finally meeting her in the parking lot where she sat wild-eyed and seething after waiting for hours in our un-air-conditioned car.

Articulating each word through clenched teeth, a skill I still hope to one day master, she'd promise that I was never, *ever*, going back. Ever. Something that would slip her mind by the following year, when I'd do it all over again.

Unwavering in my devotion to theme parks, I eventually honeymooned at Disney and once my kids were old enough, they, too, were indoctrinated.

Somewhere between the age of twenty-five and having to eat dinner before dark, however, my tolerance for rides, of any kind, evaporated into thin air; not unlike my eyesight, ability to recall movie titles, and a distinguishable waistline.

I discovered this on a sweltering July day back in the early 2000s after taking our young daughters to spend the day at Six Flags.

It started off well enough.

We walked around, watched the kiddie shows, and did the usual stuff.

Being ride enthusiasts, my husband and I even took a few solo turns on the big roller coasters between taking the kids on the more family-friendly amusements.

And, just because I could, I indulged in a few of my favorite fair delicacies, including a couple of frozen Cokes, pepperoni pizza, chocolate Dippin' Dots, fried dough, part of a burger, and several handfuls of my daughter's fries.

It was on The Balloon Race, a seemingly innocent ride in which occupants enjoy soaring "up, up, and away" in a faux, hot-air balloon, that whooshes round, round, round, and around, and around, and around, again, that I realized I wasn't feeling so good.

Swaying slightly as I disembarked, I signaled to my husband, telling him in a panicked whisper, that I was at DEFCON 1 on the nausea scale and without immediate intervention, it was going to be nuclear.

A frantic gift shop search produced an unexpected miracle: a travel-sized pack of Pepto-Bismol which, all things considered, should probably be sold in bulk near the corndogs and upside-down rides.

Somehow, I managed to choke down the chalky pills in hopes of averting disaster.

But I was already too far gone.

A sainted martyr in Keds, I reassured my husband and kids that I was fine, insisted they go on a few more rides, and told them to meet me at the car.

Queasy, stumbling, and sweating profusely, I barely made it past the park gates.

Unable to go any further, I gave up and stretched out on the sidewalk next to a garbage can.

I laid immobilized for what seemed like hours as people walked by, looking at me suspiciously as they dumped their empty soda cups into the trash.

Sometime later my husband and kids arrived and nearly kept going, thinking I was some unfortunate patron who'd had one too many at the beer tent, before recognizing the orange t-shirt and shorts I'd left the house in that morning.

They helped me to the car, and we began the hour-long ride home.

Merely five minutes in, we had to pullover in a grassy church parking lot filled with folks just getting out of a service.

I crawled to shady spot under a tree while my husband nervously stood a few feet away, unsure of Sick-Spouse- In-Church-Grass protocol, while the kids cried in the car.

A couple sitting at a nearby picnic table hurriedly collected their belongings and moved to another spot.

In a testament to my strong constitution, I succeeded in keeping the contents of my stomach from becoming a public exhibition and eventually made it home.

I'd like to say that I learned a valuable lesson that day about the inherent dangers of mixing Dippin'Dots and amusement rides and that I never did it again.

But I hate to lie.

The Dentist

I DON'T LIKE THE DENTIST. HOWEVER, AS RECOMMENDED, I TRY to go every six months. Mostly because I like the idea of my teeth being inside my mouth and not in a cup on the nightstand. So, I do what I can.

Half the time I don't even remember that I have an appointment. I'm pretty sure it's because the people at the front desk of my dentist's office insist that I make them so far in advance, I'm afraid I might not still be alive by the time they roll around.

Though I understand the need to book them so far out, most days I struggle to remember whether I put deodorant on or not, let alone recall a commitment I made in a different calendar year.

When I arrive, it's always the same. Even if I'm on time, I still spend twenty minutes sitting in the waiting room listening to an unlucky person undergo some kind of excessive, offshore drilling procedure while I'm stuck paging through Motor Cross Digest because all the good magazines are taken.

No matter how often I go, I always have to start with X-Rays. Other than discovering Jimmy Hoffa buried beneath my left molar, I'm not sure what they think they're going to find that's significant enough to warrant repeated shots of radiation directly to my head.

And with all the advances in modern technology, you'd think they would have figured out by now how to shape dental X-Rays to actually fit in your mouth. Honestly, how difficult can this be?

Yet the hygienist inserts little paper-covered razor blades into every crevice of my mouth while I'm expected to grip them with my teeth without blinking, breathing, or crying for help while she takes the pictures.

Once finished, we move on the main event.

When you think about it, there's something humbling about reclining in a chair, mouth stretched open, while someone else scrapes encrusted plaque off the back of your teeth. I imagine it's similar to how my cat feels when the vet takes his temperature.

If that's not bad enough, the hygienist then uses my paper bib to wipe off anything disgusting she fishes out in the process, leaving me no choice but to look down at what equates to a Picasso of my poor dental hygiene for the rest of the appointment.

However, it pales in comparison to having my teeth polished.

I know they've heard of toothpaste at my dentist's office, so I don't understand why they still use that stuff that comes in a color even Crayola won't name and tastes like drywall cement mixed with gravel.

I can't get it out of my mouth fast enough. But that's a problem, too, because apparently, I lack the skillset necessary to spit into dental sink next to my chair. Instead, I end up slobbering it out in a display of ropey saliva and tooth polish that I end up wiping on my sleeve.

When it's over, a second hygienist comes in and one of them sticks a tiny, metal pitchfork in and out of my gums while the other writes down numbers. I get some ones. A few twos. They exchange looks when there are a couple of fives. I can only assume this means that I have catastrophic gum disease caused by too much Kool-Aid and saltwater taffy.

But I find that hard to believe.

In fact, in the last few visits I've been told that much like my bra size and checking account, my gums are suffering from recession. They say it's probably from over-brushing and that I'm eventually going to need gum surgery. From what I gather, it involves removing skin from the roof of my mouth and reattaching it to the problem area.

While I've given the idea careful consideration, I've decided that I'd rather undergo a brain transplant before signing up for a "gumectomy" and am willing to go gumless for the remainder of my days if that's what is necessary to avoid it.

At the end of my visit the dentist drops in to poke around

in my mouth one last time before announcing that I have a few cracks in my teeth, but not to worry, they're due to old age. Then I'm done.

Before leaving they ask me to make another appointment. I tell them I'd like to, but that I have to update my will first.

If the Shoe Fits, Return It

AFTER COMPLETING AN INFORMAL INVENTORY OF MY CLOSET, I discovered that I own forty-one pairs of shoes.

That's a lot considering my last name isn't "Kardashian," and the only place I routinely visit is the refrigerator.

It's not like I've got a fetish where I compulsively shop for shoes in a pathetic bid to fill the empty void in my life, though if we were talking cardigan sweaters it'd be different conversation altogether.

No, far from being a shoe enthusiast, I'm a shoe atheist, believing that a shoe that is both comfortable and stylish doesn't exist.

Even so, I continue searching in the event I'm mistaken, and that when I die, it'll be wearing shoes I actually like.

That, however, is doubtful.

From Marshalls to Macy's, I've spent decades canvasing retailers in hopes of scoring the elusive, Perfect Pair.

One that doesn't pinch, chafe, scrape, bind, deform, torment, or torture my crusty, middle-aged feet, yet avoids looking like something I picked up at the medical supply store.

It's an ongoing pursuit requiring persistence and patience, especially if I'm shopping at a discount retailer on the weekend.

Clogging up the Size Seven aisle, carts parked directly in the middle, are all the other frenzied women without functional footwear, eager to discover the Perfect Pair among the Made-Exclusively-for-Bridge-Club Sketchers, and pretty-but-painful, harem sandals covered in fake jewels.

A hopeless cause, of course, because even if they existed, they'd already be in someone else's closet and not on a shelf surrounded by a mob of irritable, desperate women, all wearing disposable nylon peds because they forgot to bring socks.

Despite knowing that there's no chance of finding the

Perfect Pair, I still bring home at least one box of "These Could Work" shoes, even though they're almost always the wrong size, color, and brand.

I know better than to wear the These Could Work shoes immediately for fear of rendering them unreturnable.

Instead, I keep them in the box for at least a week, where I study them, occasionally try them on (carpet only), until, eventually, I feel they're ready for official ownership.

Once I'm sure, *really* sure, I commit and wear them out of the house, usually on an extended day trip that requires walking forty city blocks just to find a club sandwich because my husband says it's too nice out to take a taxi.

It doesn't take long before realizing that my These Could Work shoes are, in reality, "911" shoes, when wearing them is more agonizing than undergoing bunion surgery without anesthetic.

Despite qualifying for hell-on-earth status, I still put them back in my closet when I get home, used Band-Aids and all, because I bought them and Woman Law states that shoes must be kept until infinity in case an occasion comes up that they're perfect for, regardless of how much they hurt. The end.

Though I suffer from profound shoe anxiety, I can't compete with my mom, who has turned buying and returning shoes into a fulltime career.

Insisting that a pair of four-year-old Asics are the only shoes that ever have - or ever will - fit her feet, she's tirelessly pursued finding another pair exactly like them, only to come up empty-footed.

But that hasn't discouraged her.

Insisting she can tell whether or not shoes fit just by the country they were manufactured in; my mom doesn't even try most of them on.

When she does, they immediately hurt the bone spur on her big toe, do not offer EVEN CLOSE to enough arch support, or are way too loose.

I've tried pointing out that if she just tied the laces a bit tighter, the last problem, at least, could be remedied.

But it doesn't matter, because she's already made up her mind, packaged them up, and shipped them back up to Zappos, which is likely operating a special distribution center just to keep up with her orders.

Delivering and picking up packages daily, I'm pretty sure the UPS guy suspects that she's operating some kind of sophisticated shoe cartel, smuggling Asics through a tunnel located beneath her 55-and-over community and distributing them on the black sneaker market.

Fortunately, I'm not at that point yet, since among the 41 pairs I own, there are at least a couple that get the job done, even if I don't actually like them.

And, if nothing more, I'm holding out hope for number 42.

I want to believe.

Friends Say the Darndest Things

WHEN I WAS TWELVE, MY BEST FRIEND TOLD ME THAT OF ALL THE sixth graders at Kennedy Elementary School, I had the biggest butt.

While I admittedly had some extra square footage in the basement as a prepubescent, and could likely fit a pool table on it even now, there were at least a couple of other people more deserving of the award, even if I did qualify for honorable mention.

In high school, a different friend cleverly modified the words to the old Hollies song, "Long, Tall, Woman in a Black Dress," and instead sang the words, *short, fat, woman in a black dress* to me as we were getting ready to go out one night.

To be fair, after telling her to go casual, I broke out a dress I could've been worn to the Oscars hoping to one-up her with a "Oh, this old thing? I found it in the back of my closet."

Even though I probably deserved it, thirty years later the refrain still plays in my head every time I pull on a black dress or if I hear the song on the radio.

I can't help but wonder why my menopausal memory loss, which has been so efficient in ensuring that I routinely forget most appointments along with anything vital at the grocery store, hasn't seen fit to erase a snarky comment made before I was old enough to vote.

Regardless, I've since earned the right to vote and according to a long-time friend, my hair has too.

While out to dinner recently, she looked at me over the breadbasket before bluntly declaring, "Your hair is so…adult."

Confused, I asked what she meant.

"Well, you know," she said, "before your hair was kind of messy. And now it's… adult."

This same person once told me, without preamble, that

I smelled like bologna. And on a separate occasion asked me, across a room full of people, if I was wearing a bra, because either way it didn't look like it.

Immediately following, I purchased some padded bras. And after giving the "adult" hair some thought, I've concluded that it's probably not a bad thing that my messy tresses have now earned the right to enlist in the military, legally buy alcohol and maybe apply for a mortgage.

Still, based on her comment, it's hard to know if I was channeling Medusa prior to my last salon appointment, or if my latest haircut makes me look like Betty White.

I've learned that friends aren't the only ones happy to provide uninvited feedback. Family members are just as eager to offer up their unfiltered thoughts.

Not long ago, my dad studied me before telling me that as I've aged, I look more and more like his deceased aunts.

I'm not sure how to take this considering the only picture I've ever seen of them is a grainy photo of some angry-looking Czechoslovakian women with furrowed brows and square jawlines. And outside of the angry, furrow-browed, square-jawed part, I just don't see the resemblance.

I've doled out plenty of my own foot-in-mouth observations, too.

In middle school, I earnestly told my best friend that the only reason she liked the Eurhythmics was because she just wasn't smart enough to appreciate better music.

And my mom reminds me of the time that as a kid I barged into her room while she was getting dressed and proclaimed, "Wow. You need to lose weight."

I like to believe that I've come a long way since then and make an effort to think about what I say before it leaves my lips, just in case someone isn't actually interested in knowing my opinion on their pants-size or that I disdain their taste in music.

I also do my best to understand that, like me, people sometimes say stupid stuff without realizing that telling someone that they smell like sandwich meat might not be considered a compliment.

As far as my hair is concerned, I don't mind that it's matured. With any luck, now that it's an adult, maybe it'll help pay some bills.

Gainful Employment

I'M NOT AFRAID OF HARD WORK.

In fact, I've almost always had a job, unless shopping and petting the cat don't count.

Like many pre-teens I began my career at eleven, babysitting the neighbor kids.

As part of the gig, I was expected to bathe, dress, feed and entertain the tots, as well as clean the house, cook meals and do the dishes, even if they weren't mine.

All for $1.00 an hour.

Considering that I've done all those things for the last twenty-five years, free of charge, it doesn't seem like such a bad deal.

Anyway, by the time I turned thirteen, I was ready for "real" work and decided to detassel corn.

Common in the Midwest, detasseling is an agricultural job where teams of kids are shuttled to farms in order to pluck the tops off from corn stalks, preventing pollination or violating child labor laws. I'm not sure which, but probably both.

Regardless, my brother spent three summers detasseling, earning him a new Pentax camera one year and a lime green Volkswagen Rabbit the next.

Eager to earn some worthwhile cash of my own, I signed up.

On the first 100-degree day in July, I filled a grocery bag with potato chips, a thermos of Kool-Aid, and boarded a bus at dawn.

Despite being surrounded by all the country kids that didn't speak to me during the school year, I was excited, contemplating how I was going to spend my paycheck.

Besides, I was one of them now. We'd work the fields together. In harmony. Comradery among the corn.

Upon arriving, I was assigned a row and instructed to walk at a clipped pace, removing tassels in sync with the other workers.

It seemed easy enough.

Until it wasn't.

The combination of wet stalks and tropical heat almost immediately gave me a rash and pulling tassels proved to be harder than I expected. There were also insects crawling all over the corn.

A lot of them.

Scratching and slapping, I began to run, feeling faint, tripping in the dirt, and missing most of the stalks in a frenzied attempt to reach the end.

In the span of forty-five minutes, my agricultural career began and ended.

Once old enough, I picked up a job at the local fast-food joint.

I nearly quit on the spot after discovering that I had to wear a brown polyester jumpsuit with orange stripes and matching visor.

Instead, in a desperate bid to make it more stylish, I had it altered.

A decision I'd come to regret.

With dominion over all living creatures and the drive-thru window, Deb, my shift supervisor, wielded her authority like a razor-sharp scythe.

Sensing that I'd never adequately scoop fries, she disliked me from the get-go and made sure to put me on the bun oven whenever I worked.

Upon noticing the alterations, her face grew red and blotchy, and in nothing short of fury Deb demanded to know who gave me permission to modify the company uniform.

Since we both knew no one had, I felt like it was sort of a trick question.

But she didn't fire me. Instead, on a journey of personal exploration, she opted to see what it would take to get me to quit.

In the weeks that followed I found myself cleaning out the drain of the men's urinal, razor-blading gum from beneath chairs, and mopping up soda from the bottom of dirty garbage cans.

When that didn't work, she tasked me with wiping down the baseboards that ran around the restaurant floor.

Though it doesn't sound too bad, Deb had me do it immediately following my high school's homecoming football game.

With hordes of my classmates ordering food and jammed into every free booth, I crawled under feet and tables with my bucket and brush, scrubbing the tile paneling until the job was done.

I didn't quit. In fact, I worked there until leaving for college nearly a year later.

In the end, my determination earned Deb's grudging respect and we became friends.

A complete lie, of course. We hated each other right up until the day I left.

However, I did eventually move up the ranks to work the drive-thru window, a small victory if nothing else.

I'm not sure whatever became of Deb, but hope that wherever she is, she's working the bun oven.

Mirror, Mirror

ON A RECENT VACATION I DISCOVERED AN EXTRATERRESTRIAL in the bathroom of my hotel.

In the dim lighting provided by the same folks who outfit parking garages, I could see it standing by the sink. With dimply skin, wiry hair and squinty eyes, it wore the same startled expression as me.

Terrified, I watched as it stepped into the shower and nearly screamed before realizing that I was looking at myself.

And then I really did want to scream because I couldn't decide if I actually look that scary in real life or if Hilton orders their bathroom mirrors from Spirit Halloween store.

I'm guessing the former because the hotel thing wasn't my first close encounter. In fact, I have one almost every time I go shopping. I'm not sure what it is about dressing rooms but trying on clothes almost always feels like an alien abduction.

First, I have to stand in line while some grumpy attendant does a cavity inspection to ensure I haven't stuffed a down-filled parka into my bra. Then I'm handed a number and sent down a long fluorescent corridor.

From there, I squeeze into a tiny vestibule where I remove my clothes under hot, interrogation lights and squeeze into things that don't belong to me, followed by an out-of-body experience in which I have to look at myself in them. All while listening to Mariah Carey feel her emotions.

Finally, before leaving, my memory is mysteriously neutralized because I always end up buying something that nobody in their right mind would ever wear, with no recollection of ever having purchased it.

Sure, there are a handful of retailers that use trickery like elongated mirrors and soft, flattering lights to persuade me that I look good in yoga pants. They're the same stores that sell my favorite jeans two sizes smaller than I normally wear while still fitting over my kneecaps. I'm a rewards member at all of them.

But as small as my fictitious size appears, it's still enormous compared to the new, smaller sizes apparel companies keep coming out with.

I'm not sure how much further they can go. I mean, after 0 and 00 what else is there? Pants sized to the negative power? Granule? Particle? Atom?

It doesn't matter; I'm okay with deception. I lie to myself every day. I convince myself that the jeans I bought after a successful period of food depravation still fit despite a prolonged pasta bender. Even if putting them on is like trying to get toothpaste back in the tube.

And if closing the top button means temporarily cutting off the blood supply to my upper body, I'll do it as long as I can get them up. God forbid someone throws them in the wash, renewing their elasticity and effectively ruining days of stretching them into a wearable size.

A few years ago, I got my act together and committed to regular exercise and eating healthy. After many months of discipline and hard work, I lost twenty pounds and never felt better. Flushed with success I went to purchase a new swimsuit to show off my results.

Standing in the dressing room I saw what my own bathroom mirror had neglected to tell me. Despite all my efforts, I did not look like a Victoria's Secret model.

I just looked like me. A thinner, nominally better version of me, but with the same lumps and bulges I always had, and no one was going to strap wings to my back and send me down the catwalk anytime soon.

It took everything I had to not to drive directly to the grocery store, buy a carton of Little Debbie Snack Cakes, and eat them all while watching "Sleepless in Seattle."

I fought the urge and instead bought a suit that boasts hidden panels and is made from the same material as latex balloons. It's not perfect, but then again neither am I. And, hopefully, as long as I cover my eyes in hotel bathrooms and order my clothes online, my future close encounters will be limited to movie theaters.

Auld Lang Syne

UNLIKE MOST PEOPLE, I DON'T COMMEMORATE NEW YEAR'S ON January 1st. Instead it falls on the last Wednesday in August when my kids go back to school.

Though I'm usually excited when they come home for the summer, at some point midway through July they turn into houseguests who have outstayed their welcome. Sleeping past noon, leaving a trail of dirty dishes and laundry in their wake, I want them out like uninvited squatters whose sole purpose in life is to eat chips down to the crumbs before stuffing the bag back in the pantry.

The week before school begins, the countdown kicks off when it becomes painfully obvious that despite repeated nagging, neither kid has bothered to do the summer homework which usually involves reading and producing a dissertation on a 1000-page book on quantum physics that even Bill Gates couldn't pull off in three days.

Then, because of back-to-school martial law, a Target pilgrimage is required in order to purchase excessive amounts of school supplies they insist they NEED before it even begins. All of which are rendered obsolete on the first day when teachers tell students what they actually need.

This invariably results in the 8:58 p.m. drug store dash for binders and book covers, not unlike the "I-Need-Poster-Board-For-Tomorrow Crisis," that occurs at least twice during the calendar school year.

Also necessary is the purchase of a graphing calculator, not to be confused with the scientific calculator. Despite the fact the both appear capable of computing the gross domestic product in Slovenia and cost at least as much as my last car, they are apparently not the same and cannot be reused in consecutive years, for any reason.

Ever.

Since I didn't even learn how to do fractions until sixth grade, I don't understand why my kids require a calculator with buttons including the symbol that Prince changed his name to and wonder if it's actually being used in a sinister plot to upload human DNA to the government.

Though I'm not sure how it works for boys, as the parent of two teenage daughters, back-to-school requires that I purchase them both entirely new wardrobes and shoes with no regard to necessity.

I always hope that our annual field trip to the overcrowded mall is going to play out like a fun movie montage where my girls try on funny hats as Van Morrison's "Brown Eyed Girl" plays in the background.

Instead it's more like an episode of "Say Yes to the Dress," complete with brawls, ugly crying, dressing room confrontations over size, style, and budget, along with my repeated objections that unless they're going on tour with Madonna, they're not allowed to dress like her.

In the aftermath, there's barely enough money left in my checking account to buy a roll of Lifesavers and I'm left wondering why I bankrupted myself to buy sweaters and winter coats while it's still hot enough outside to be burned at the stake without matches.

Despite that, they usually wear the sweaters on the first day anyway. I'm guessing it's hereditary.

Not unlike my daughters, I decided to wear my new Esprit long-sleeve shirt and thick canvas pants on the first day of eighth grade, a fiery Midwest day in late August. Fifteen minutes into my hour-long bus ride home, I was cooking like a four-alarm fire. Instead of being a fashion statement, my fancy brand-name outfit was nothing short of a near-death experience and I learned a valuable lesson that day about mixing ego and climatology.

But I can't be held responsible for decisions made during puberty. Around that same time, I also sported the Barbra Streisand, "A Star is Born," perm, forever preserved in my school pictures, which always seemed to be taken on the most inconvenient day of the year.

Along with the perm, Mac McGoon Portrait Studios also immortalized the time I suffered from an acute case of chapped lips and had a perfect circle of raw, red skin above *and* below my lips, as well as the Bad Acne Year, and the time I shaved off my left eyebrow in a personal grooming accident.

Lucky for my daughters, photos today can be retouched and edited to ensure that no matter what they look like on the day school pictures are taken, they won't look like themselves.

I'll recognize them, of course. They'll be the ones wearing sweaters.

Driver's Ed

I think that I'm a good driver. I've never really had an accident except for the time my husband left the garbage can in the middle of our driveway and I backed into it.

Of course, he argues that it was off to the side, but I'm fairly confident that it wasn't because, obviously, how else could I have hit it?

He also points out that if I had backed over a pedestrian instead, it wouldn't matter whether they were in the middle of the road or not, it would still be my fault.

Though I don't exactly follow the logic, for the sake of diplomacy I've agreed to disagree on whom, exactly, is to blame for his negligence.

Besides, after he reversed out of the garage a couple of years ago and plowed directly into a car parked in our driveway, I don't really think my husband can use the whole Pedestrian versus Garbage Can theory anymore, anyway.

Minor mishaps aside, we hardly compare to a lot of other people on the road.

Sometimes, when I contemplate how many unqualified drivers have been given legal permission to operate a motor vehicle, it makes me question everything I'm certain of in this world including gravity, God, and another season of "Dancing with the Stars."

Fortunately, I've developed a primer to help classify them into a few, easy categories, beginning with The Multitasker.

Texting, eating, putting on makeup, rock polishing; there's nothing The Multitasker can't do while operating heavy machinery at seventy-five miles an hour.

WAY too busy to set aside even a few extra minutes to accomplish normal tasks at home, the Multitasker takes them on the road where things like looking out the windshield, merging, and vehicular homicide are merely afterthoughts.

Fortunately, they are usually easy to spot as they swerve all over the road, attempting to pull on pantyhose and steer at the same time.

With no plausible explanation, The Left-Laner clogs up the passing lane, guaranteeing that every single driver stuck behind them is obliged to maintain whatever speed they have deemed appropriate for that particular stretch of highway, hence forth.

Skillful motorists, Left-Laners are practiced at sustaining the exact same speed as the car next to them in the travel lane, preventing any sort of sneaky, right-lane, passing maneuvers in an attempt to break ranks. There's little hope for escape once The Left-Laner has arrived on the scene and no one's getting home early.

It's important not to confuse The Left-Laner with The No-Laner, someone who struggles with commitment issues.

Your lane, their lane, the shoulder, doesn't really matter. No-Laners drift all over the road, nearly sideswiping you, before idly heading back over to their side or riding it out on the center line for a while, before eventually gliding back into a lane again, leaving you in a cold sweat trying to guess which side of the road they'll end up on next.

The Pass-Competer cruises at normal speed in the right lane; until you try and get around them.

Pass-Competers consider this an aggressive move on your part and will not allow you to initiate passing without first applying a heavy foot to the gas to ensure that it doesn't come easy, if at all.

Even if you succeed, you haven't seen the last of them. Threatened that you've taken the lead, The Pass-Competer inevitably floors it to get around you and once safely back out front, they immediately slow back down, starting the entire process all over again.

When the grill of the car behind me is no longer visible in my rearview mirror, I know that I'm being followed by The

Proctologist; someone who is one brake tap away from performing my next colonoscopy.

The Proctologist has no regard for personal space and could care less if you are leaving a trail of fire or sonic boom in your wake, it still isn't fast enough. Unfortunately, there's not much that can be done about The Proctologist except to ask them if they mind checking for polyps the next time they're riding your license plate.

Finally, there's The VIP.

Typically found behind the wheel of a black, Taj Mah-Suburban with a cell phone attached to their head, VIP's largely consider traffic laws as beneath them, and do not acknowledge other motorists on road.

The only course of action when The VIP approaches is to quickly move out of the way or risk certain death as they drive over your car on their way to the gym.

And, as I already explained, I'm The Perfect Driver. Enough said.

Crime and Punishment

WHEN MY DAUGHTERS WERE BOTH UNDER THE AGE OF FIVE, I made the mistake of thinking I could take them to the mall on a crowded Saturday afternoon without consequence.

While it seemed like a good idea at the time, in hindsight it was more like deciding to take a bottle of laxatives before embarking on a cross-country road trip.

After refusing to purchase the entire contents of the Disney Store, the result was instant hysteria, with my older daughter laying on the floor and shrieking like a civil defense siren warning of an impending comet strike.

When the whole let's-calm-down-before-someone-calls-the-police tactic didn't work, I switched to shushing and pleading, before finally throwing in the towel and giving her a time-out.

Within moments, a super-helpful woman came over and pointedly told me that I was wrong for penalizing my daughter in public before walking away in a huff.

I was surprised.

When I was a kid, being required to sit quietly on a mall bench for thirty seconds to reflect on my behavior was the least of my worries.

Growing up, instead of the more popular corporal punishment, my parents preferred to discipline us with what they considered "logical" consequences.

Any time my brother or I did something wrong, which usually amounted to some type of screaming match over who had to change the channel on the TV, my parents leveraged it to accomplish a household task too egregious to impose under ordinary circumstances.

It didn't take much.

With bionic hearing, my mom would know if we were

arguing, even if it was in the basement of the neighbor's house, a half mile away.

The response was swift, predictable and the obvious disciplinary choice to a heated dispute.

Weed the driveway.

Sure, it probably doesn't sound like a big deal.

Except that instead of a normal paved road, our driveway was massive, circular, and made entirely of gravel. When there wasn't snow, it amounted to a quarry pit full of weeds and moss that proliferated between every. Single. Stone.

It was the equivalent of attempting to harvest only the white grains from a pail of sand.

The Weeding of the Driveway could be exacted at any time, but was almost always imposed in July or August, when the weeds were at their worst, humidity at its highest, and grasshoppers most likely to find their way up my shorts.

My mom would insist that we begin at opposite ends until finally meeting in the middle when we were done.

Though it sounds like some kind of teaching-moment metaphor, it was more about maximizing the ground we could cover, as well as keeping us separated in order to minimize the risk that we'd argue further while pulling chickweed from impacted stone.

We argued anyway, as the distance wasn't nearly enough to compensate for our seething anger over whose fault it was that we were stuck doing it in the first place.

We also fought over what station to play on the radio we set between us in order to listen to a barely-audible Paul McCartney sing about silly love songs.

It wasn't worth it since we almost always got caught and a follow-up punishment to the original punishment was levied (Trouble x Trouble = Trouble ^{2}), meaning that once the driveway was complete, we'd move on to the brick patios, both flourishing weed gardens lying in wait for sibling tensions to boil over.

Weeding wasn't the only consequence in my house.

If one of us accidentally forgot to the shut the door behind us when we left, it carried a mandatory sentence of repetitively opening and closing that door to help encourage remembering.

You'd think that doing it 500 times would be incentive enough to never forget. And yet it wasn't.

We'd have company over for dinner and I'd be stuck standing in the hallway, attached to the door, 171, 172, 173, 174...

It takes a long time to open and close a door 500 times.

Eventually, I learned and rarely - if ever - do I leave doors in my own house open.

For any reason.

My kids do sometimes. But I wouldn't dream of making them do that.

However, we have a walkway leading to the front door that's begun to sprout weeds up through the bricks.

It's only a matter of time before they argue.

The Waiting Room

LIKE PRETTY MUCH EVERYONE ELSE, I DON'T ENJOY GOING TO the doctor.

No matter what the reason.

Even if my physician was moonlighting as lottery commissioner and I held the winning Powerball ticket, I still wouldn't want to go.

Just making an appointment is a lesson in fortune telling, requiring a crystal ball to predict my plans on a Tuesday afternoon, twelve months in the future, when most days I can't even figure out what I'm doing for lunch.

After nailing down a day I could possibly show up, we enter into a game of Timeslot Go Fish.

"Do you have anything at 10:00 a.m.?"

No. Go fish.

"Can you come at 4:15 p.m.?"

Too late. Go fish.

"Is Monday available?"

Completely booked. Go fish.

"What about the following week?"

I'm on vacation. Go fish.

Once someone wins, I forget to write it down, remembering only when I get the reminder call the day before and am forced to reschedule, starting the whole thing all over again.

As the date of the appointment closes in, I become paralyzed by Doctor Scale Anxiety.

Not only do doctor scales make me feel like I'm being weighed in at a 4H livestock contest, but despite stripping off my clothes, shoes and not using any hairspray, they inexplicably read at least fifteen pounds more than the one in my bathroom.

As the nurse notches the weight bar over, over, then over again before stopping on a number we didn't agree on, I resist the urge to appeal the verdict by shrieking, "*Lies! All lies!*" and instead confess my addiction to double-stuffed Oreos so we can move on.

Immediately following confirmation of my catastrophic weight gain, the nurse takes my blood pressure, which is off the charts due to the confirmation of my catastrophic weight gain, then we sit in silence while she types it all into my permanent record.

Because I've usually consumed a bucket of coffee on my way to the appointment, I'm forced to prematurely use the bathroom while still in the waiting room, leaving me unable to perform the task later when handed a plastic cup and sent down the hall.

I try anyway, using the time to contemplate if the last person who used the black, Sharpie marker to identify their cup, did so before—or after—filling it up.

After admitting defeat, I'm led to a room where time grinds to halt as I page through two-year-old magazines or blatantly ignore the "NO CELL PHONES" sign taped to the wall to pre-emptively look up what might be wrong with me on WebMD, in case my doctor wants a second opinion.

In some awkward state of undress, I sit on the table, trying not to move a lot since the crinkly, white paper it's covered with makes me feel like I'm one tomato and some shredded lettuce away from being a to-go sandwich.

If nothing more, I'm grateful to be in my own space instead of the waiting room, where no matter what remote corner I sit in, someone who appears to have a raging case of Bob Costas pink eye parks it in the chair next to me, regardless if every other seat in the place is empty.

Not unlike Movie Theater Law, which governs that even if there's not another living soul there, someone will come last minute, sit directly behind me, and spend the entire time tearing the plastic off a box of Junior Mints or talk nonstop until the last credit rolls.

When the doctor finally knocks on the door, I'm usually so grateful someone didn't forget about me that I don't mind that we're probably going to have to do something objectionable with a sharp utensil or at the very least, a large cotton swab.

Both are preferable, however, to any questions my doctor might ask about how often I exercise, how many glasses of wine I drink per day and what the deal is with double-stuffed Oreos.

I guess it doesn't really matter, since I have no intention of answering any of them honestly and am only stalling until my doctor checks the clock and rushes out the door to examine Bob Costas.

Once dressed again, I realize I have to go to the bathroom.

Having already inspected the Sharpie, I wait until I get home.

Seven Days Out

Like a gazelle sensing a predator among the herd, my husband becomes still and unblinking after I mention my plans to do a diet detox.

Though he feigns interest, I smell his fear and imagine one of those red, weather tickers scrolling behind his eyes as he awaits further instructions on whether to head for the basement or simply evacuate.

It's not the first time I've proposed going on some new diet. From the Mediterranean to South Beach, I've pretty much tried them all. Unlike the exotic destinations they're named after, however, the experience has never proven to be exciting or luxurious, and to date, no one has served me drinks by the pool while on one of them.

While I'm not really a fasting or detox sort of person, with the arrival of clothes-too-small-for-me season, I decide to embark on a celebrity-style "detox" that promises to remove toxins, cleanse my system (though I could argue that one serving of edamame does roughly the same thing in a lot less time), and help drop a few pounds.

To be fair, outside of donuts, bacon, and handfuls of Christmas cookies, I eat pretty well. But there's always room for improvement, including curbing my afternoon cheese and cracker date with the Gallo brothers and giving the frozen yogurt shops a chance to fill up someone else's reward card.

And there's the caffeine thing.

I live for my morning coffee, or as I like to call it, "The Elixir of Life."

Without at least two cups, my family has learned the hard way to avoid all communication unless someone's on fire or Harrison Ford is at the front door.

Since my detox of choice calls for the elimination of refined sugar, gluten, dairy, meat, alcohol, and caffeine for seven days, I can't blame my husband for being afraid.

He should move.

I first check with my doctor, who recommends that instead of drinking water mixed with cayenne pepper for a week, I simply make a few changes and detox in moderation as opposed to adopting the Beyoncé method since it's probably not healthy. And, also, I'm not Beyoncé.

Motivated and armed with my detox list, I hit the grocery store. Nearly two hundred dollars later I realize that detoxing isn't cheap and wonder if I shouldn't have just bought new clothes instead.

Amid the regular items in my fridge and pantry, the new additions of almond milk and flax seed stand out like foreigners in a small town. I'm not even sure what flax seed is. The first time I add them to a smoothie (for protein and fiber apparently), I spend the rest of the day picking them out of my teeth.

Otherwise, the first couple days are surprisingly tolerable. Despite feeling mildly hung-over from lack of caffeine, I manage to function on herbal tea in the morning. I also survive my new regimen of fresh produce and brown rice without coming completely unglued. I decide that detoxing isn't so bad and if wanted to, I could probably even fast for a few days.

That all changes on day three, when, after stopping to get gas, I realize my husband has used up all my grocery store gas points. Through a hungry, red haze, I send him an all-caps text, laced with expletives and threaten to call him at work to discuss it further. We both understand there will be consequences.

It's possible that I'm irritable.

By day five, I'm reduced to smelling empty coffee cups in the sink and watching Food Network round the clock. No one is allowed to discuss eating or permitted to enter the kitchen.

But I also learn that I'm supposed to grind up the flax seed instead of eating it whole and discover that it's not so bad.

As I close out the final days of the detox, I notice that remarkably, I do, sort of, feel better. Nothing profound or anything, just better. I check the scale, and I've lost three pounds.

On day eight, I eat steak, ice cream and invite Ernest and Julio over to celebrate.

But a funny thing happens on day nine. I wake up and have a fruit smoothie with flax seed.

And make coffee, too. I'm not crazy.

Grocery Store Jeopardy

GOING TO THE GROCERY STORE MAKES ME ANGRY. IN FACT, I'M often mad before I pass through the sliding doors.

It usually begins with my inability to effectively park my car in the lot.

Stricken with age-related parking anxiety, I find it impossible to fit between the lines, forcing me to pull in and back up multiple times just to avoid being jack-knifed next to the carriage return.

Despite repeated attempts, it happens anyway, making it seem like I'm that person who thinks my decade-old, dented car is worthy of two spots, as opposed to the allotted, one.

It doesn't help that I drive a seven-seater minivan, which for someone with my limited grasp of physics, is like trying to land the space shuttle on a postage stamp.

And while seeking a spot, there's always at least one near collision with a Backer-Inner.

This uber-efficient individual, who has to back into any given parking spot no matter what, does a hard slam of the brakes directly in front of me, with no warning whatsoever, before leisurely backing into the spot I'd been eyeballing. Sometimes the Backer-Inner backs in and out a second time get it *juuussst* right, sending me into a complete Suburban Mom meltdown.

Once 'parked,' I just make it to the entrance before remembering my collection of mismatched reusable bags, requiring the walk of shame back to the car to retrieve them from the back seat.

Arriving at the doors for a second time, I never manage to score the convenient, midsized cart.

Instead, I'm stuck with the dump truck version, jammed tight into the cart in front of it.

Too lazy to pick another, I waste valuable time jerking them forward and back as the Backer-Inner, clutching a coupon organizer, hovers impatiently behind me.

Upon liberation, it becomes apparent that I've unwisely selected the one with the janky side-wheel or dirty Purell wipe left in the bottom, adding Finding a Trash Can to the job.

By the time I'm finally set to roll, I remember my grocery list.

Still sitting in the passenger seat.

Unable to recall a single thing on it, my surgical strike instantly becomes a game of Grocery Store Jeopardy, where every aisle equates to a category and question that I have no idea how to answer.

I'll take Dairy Products That I'm Critically Low On for $100, Alex.

Answer: This daily staple is required for coffee and cereal.

Alex, what is sour cream?

Ooooh. Sorry, no. The question is: What is milk? Milk.

Flying without a wingman, I attempt to remember what I'm out of.

It's futile, as no amount of visualization or concentrating until smoke tendrils escape from my ears, can produce even one relevant item.

Instead, I rebuy all the stuff I'm not out of and have no need for, like cream of mushroom soup and cat box liners, rendering the entire trip useless.

Navigating the aisles, I typically encounter the person who's abandoned their cart smack dab in the middle, with no regard to blocking traffic as they ponder whether to buy Del Monte fruit cocktail or the generic version.

I wish I was assertive enough to speak up.

However, my Midwest upbringing forbids any type of communication that doesn't involve apologizing for having done nothing wrong, which is, of course, what I do when they finally notice I'm waiting to get by.

On the upside, there's always the checkout line, which,

according to my husband, was designed specifically with me in mind.

I can't argue.

If there's something I don't need, I want to buy it.

Merchandized correctly, I can be persuaded that without purchasing a mini lint roller, life isn't worth living.

There are other treasures too. Double-A batteries, lighters, flash drives, and gift cards to places I'd go. If I had a gift card.

And waiting in line gives me a chance to catch up on the latest headlines.

Without all the informative magazines and papers, I'd never know a computer virus had spread to humans or that a severed leg hopped to the hospital in search of its owner.

I'd also miss out on why my breasts could be feeling neglected, forty styles guaranteed to make me look thinner, and Betty White's sad, final days.

Fortunately, I don't really have to worry about being out of the loop. As long as my list is in the passenger seat, I know I'll be back.

Me Time

I HAVE SEVERAL FRIENDS WHO PROFESS THAT THEY ENJOY VISITS to the salon or spa.

They refer to it as "Me Time."

I find this confusing since, in my world, Me Time typically involves lodging on the couch in a hair-covered bathrobe while binge-watching "Downton Abbey," and eating something smothered in gravy.

If I'm feeling especially indulgent, I'll mix in some online shopping from my phone before wrapping it up with a sleeve of Girl Scout cookies.

Not part of Me Time, however, is suffering through some kind of grooming ritual that involves my hair, eyebrows, hands, feet, bikini line, hot wax, scrubs, peels, or general contact with any part of my body by someone who hasn't taken me out to dinner first.

In fact, far from being Me Time, I consider most beauty treatments to be as enjoyable as getting the oil changed on my car, which, if nothing more, can usually be performed without developing feelings of inadequacy and having to make small talk.

My least favorite is probably the pedicure, an experience I liken to my annual trip to the gynecologist.

Both are tasks I wish I was capable of doing myself, are acutely embarrassing, and require me to admit that my home-care could probably use some improvement.

And neither are something I want to do during a Girl's Day Out.

Haircuts aren't much better.

Instead of being relaxing, I find that having my head sprayed by a firehose in someone else's sink reminds me of taking our childhood dog, Max, to the groomers so they could hose him down, remove the mats from his fur, and purge his overall stink before sending him home with bows on his ears.

Once finished and dripping, I'm forced into making life or death decisions on whether or not I need more layers. Something that only be determined once it's been done and too late to reconsider.

My favorite, however, is the annual addition of highlights to my hair, when aluminum foil packets sprout prolifically from my scalp, and for no less than sixty minutes, I am observed in public looking like the human version of a TV antenna.

I've also had "real" beauty treatments, too.

Back in the '90s, while staying at a fancy-pants hotel in San Francisco, I set up a spa appointment for a full-body scrub and loofa, somehow imagining that it would entail quiet music, warm lotion, and result in radiant skin.

It never occurred to me that I would have to strip down to my birthday suit for the service, but when I was ordered to take off my clothes and wrap up in a towel, panic set in.

The attendant reassured me that she'd done the exact same treatment on Whoopi Goldberg and Ted Danson just the week before.

Somehow this information provided very little by way of comfort, even so, I went through with it.

Far from being the luxurious, pampering experience I hoped for, I laid on a table and had every crevice of my body scrubbed out with a Brillo pad before being sent to take a Silkwood shower, complete with tears and harsh lighting.

On our anniversary a few years ago, I set up a couple's massage for my husband and I, thinking it would be romantic.

Once settled on adjoining beds, dim lights and new-age jazz playing, I couldn't focus or relax knowing that we were naked in a dark room with two complete strangers, and wondered if before leaving, we were expected to drop our car keys in a hat.

It didn't help that my husband's masseuse suffered from a heavy-breathing problem, leaving me uncertain if we were getting the knots worked out or on the receiving end of an obscene phone call.

At the urging of a friend, I gave the massage thing another try, this time solo, and discovered that even without the heavy breather it was still the most awkward forty-five minutes of my life outside of the junior prom.

Since then, I've limited my "spa" treatments to the minimum necessary to leave the house without wearing a bag on my head.

And none of them count as Me Time.

Celebrity Snubbing

GENERALLY SPEAKING, I'M A NICE PERSON. IT HAS TO DO WITH my Midwest upbringing, which governs that even if someone goes out of their way to back over me in a pickup truck, I'm required to compliment their driving and wish them a good day while still trapped under the tires.

Sure, there are probably some people, who may or may not live with me, that might disagree.

Especially if they wake me up unexpectedly in the middle of the night or don't pick up the cat's thyroid medicine from the vet.

Also, if they forget coffee cups in my car, chew cereal too loudly, leave cabinet doors ever-so-slightly ajar, rearrange the throw pillows, or make any sort of unnecessary movements or noise in my vicinity.

Outside of that, I'm pretty easygoing.

Still, I occasionally get annoyed by little things. Once, I almost went nuclear after my husband suggested that I might be high maintenance. A pot-and-kettle comment considering that most days I have to help him pick out socks that match before he leaves for work.

While it's doubtful that I'm anything close to high maintenance, under the right circumstances, it's possible that I can be difficult.

To celebrate our daughter's 18th birthday a few years back, we took a trip to New York City. What started out as a festive December day of sightseeing, became a little less fun when the rest of the planet showed up because, apparently, the holidays are a popular time to visit.

Things took a decidedly ugly turn when a steady, cold rain began to fall.

Like a scene from some B-movie, walking down the sidewalk

turned into "Attack of the Umbrella People" with every third person hitting my face as they pushed by to get a look at Alex and his magical telescope in the Macy's holiday windows.

It didn't take long before my perfectly coiffed, beauty-pageant hair collapsed beneath the weight of rain and hairspray, sticking to my head like a soggy front-door, welcome mat.

My wool coat, perfect for a chilly day in the city or any other occasion except one that includes precipitation, soon became a hot, wet blanket, smelling an lot like my childhood dog, Max, before it was time to drop him off at the groomers for a bath.

Though we probably should have just called it and gone home, I'd made dinner reservations at a New York steakhouse I'd found on TripAdvisor and because it was my daughter's birthday, I didn't want to cancel.

Stinky, soaked and irritated, we walked 47 city blocks until finally locating the restaurant.

Coming from the opposite direction were two men who appeared to be going to the same place.

Arriving first, we walked into a crowded lobby. Jammed with uppity steakhouse patrons who didn't smell and were dressed in sleek urban finery, the two men followed us in.

Immediately intimated since we weren't wearing black and looked like we'd just finished filming an episode of "Naked and Afraid," I searched for the hostess to check in.

After spotting her, I noticed the two men that had come in after us, heading over, too.

The audacity.

Who did they think they were?

I imagined they thought they were VERY IMPORTANT New Yorkers and that they were better than us. They obviously were, but I had spent the day in the rain and no one, especially not them, was going before me.

I. Was. First.

As if someone just opened a box of Krispy Kreme's across the room, I moved swiftly, smoothly cutting them off just as they reached the hostess podium.

I shot them a smug look before excusing myself and telling the hostess that we were there first. And we had reservations.

The shorter of the two men, a blond guy with glasses, glared at me before giving the hostess a beseeching look. The other one, a tall, dark-haired guy, put his hands up, and nicely indicated that we were, in fact, first.

I gave him a saccharine smile. Yes. We were.

Unsure of what to do, the hostess looked at them. Looked at us. Noting my determined, don't-even-think-about-letting-them-go-first expression, she sighed, took my name and said we'd be seated shortly.

Pleased with myself for having thwarted the would-be cutters, I sat down and waited for our table to be ready.

Within seconds, they were being escorted inside. Seething, I prepared to "have a serious talk" with the hostess when my daughter said, "Wow, that looks a lot like Keanu Reeves."

I studied the second of the two men. He did bear a striking resemblance. Which made sense since it was.

After finally being seated, I sat low in my chair, not wanting to be identified as the person who'd been rude to Keanu Reeves, who I found out was dining with his manager before heading to a wrap party for a movie he'd finished filming in New York.

So, they were probably in a hurry.

Then again, Keanu Reeves hadn't spent the day getting battered by umbrellas in order to get a photo next to the Rockefeller Center Christmas Tree. In the rain.

And also, I was first.

Condiment Alley

IT'S RECENTLY COME TO MY ATTENTION THAT IN A HOUSEHOLD of four, generally intelligent, people, I'm apparently the only one who can figure out the highly complicated task of cleaning out the refrigerator.

It seems like a relatively easy procedure.

Open refrigerator. Inspect swampy, never-been-used, bagged lettuce for any salvageable pieces. Smell the milk. Check for mold between slices of the American cheese. Discard potatoes leftover from the previous month. Halfheartedly wipe out. Done.

But based on the fact that no one else at my house has ever even attempted it, you'd think I'd earned my Ph.D. in Refrigeratorology.

To be fair, I've never attempted to hang a light fixture, which despite lacking a degree in Scary Electricity Wiring, my husband does all the time.

It's a terrifying process that begins with him going into the basement and clicking switches along the circuit breaker, one by one, while I shout "YES" or "NO," hoping I don't get it wrong. If I do, when he goes to connect the wires in the ceiling, it'll result in his instant death.

I'm not sure how he knows which wires go together or if he's just making it up as he goes along.

Either way, I mentally go over his life insurance policy whenever we go to The Home Depot in search of a new globe light and try not to respond to texts while helping him determine if there's still a live current running through the outlet.

Considering we've successfully installed new light fixtures in most rooms of the house, and he's still around to hang them, my track record is pretty good. So far anyway.

As far as the refrigerator is concerned, I can't actually blame anyone for not wanting to clean it out. Not only does it take up a lot time, it also involves a significant amount of stressful decision making on what should stay, what's got to go and how early is too early to drink the open bottle of wine.

Much like the whole paper-or-plastic dilemma at the grocery store, it's anxiety-provoking and reminds me why my therapist is flagged as a "favorite" in my contacts.

Though I try to clean out food from meals-I-don't-remember-making as often as I can, the condiments are another story. Relegated to the door and out of sight, they may as well not exist.

Occasionally, when there's a four-alarm French fry emergency, someone will have to do a recon mission for the ketchup, which is always nearly empty, but not quite, requiring some tricky banging on the counter to get what's left inside out.

Much like the hot sauce, there's always some sort of crusty build up around the top of the ketchup that everyone is too lazy to clean. Instead it breaks off and falls into the pool mid-pour, forcing a search and rescue to get it out.

Other than the usual condiment suspects, everything else jammed into the tiny shelves is there as a direct result of an impulse buy.

A classic case of "It Looked Better at the Grocery Store," I'm often persuaded to buy something that I hope will be the single, lifechanging, barbeque / hoisin / honey / mustard / horseradish / tartar / sandwich spread to ever grace a Frigidaire.

It never is, of course, but once it's found a home on the door, there's no chance of leaving.

And the fear that it might be the one condiment we need to have on hand should anyone decide to whip up a last-minute Duck Pâté en Croûte, ensures that it'll remain a permanent resident for the rest of all time.

Beyond the collection of sauces no one will ever use, there's also an assortment of strange pickled items like peppers and other vegetable-looking things I can't identify and have no recollection of buying. Since they seemingly never go bad, they, too, are lifers.

The remaining occupants of condiment alley are Salad Dressings That No One Liked and Never Will.

From off-brand balsamic vinaigrette to Southwest raspberry chipotle-flavored ranch, a majority have been finger-tested once, determined to taste worse than paint thinner, then disregarded for eternity.

Or until we have company over for dinner, in which case, we put it out hoping that someone who doesn't mind terrible food will pour it all over their salad and finish it off so we don't have to put it back.

Ultimately, that's the real problem. No one wants to use any of the unusable condiments, but more than that, no one wants to put in the effort required to dump them down the sink. And everyone feels guilty just tossing them in the garbage because of the earth and all.

So, there they stay. Like a graveyard full of bad decisions taking up valuable real estate in the refrigerator. Waiting for me to clean it out.

I will, in time. Right after I finish helping my husband pick out a new chandelier.

Badminton Elbow

Several years ago, my husband took our kids bowling as one of those last-resort activities that parents do when all other possibilities, including miniature golf, indoor playscapes, and dropping them off at someone else's house, have all been exhausted.

A day or two after their high-octane evening of gutter balls and fashionable footwear, I noticed my husband rubbing his arm and taking Advil.

When I asked him what was wrong, he sheepishly replied that, somehow, he had managed to injure his arm while bowling.

"Let me get this straight," I said, "are you telling me that you have some kind of *bowling* injury?"

Bowling.

To be honest, according to a handful of friends and most immediate family members, compassion isn't exactly one of my superpowers. I've been known to respond "suck it up" regardless of what the thermometer says, where the blisters are, or how many Band-Aids someone has bled through.

Once, when my husband and I were skiing, he hit a patch of ice and without any warning whatsoever, became a human snowball, rolling end to end in a blur of poles and waterproof gloves, before skidding to a stop.

After ensuring that his injuries were limited to minor head trauma and a torn ACL, I broke out my cell phone and took pictures of the paramedics attending to him, before snapping a few more in the emergency room in case he wanted to create a keepsake photo book or coffee mug of our day on the slopes.

So, considering this current injury was the result of a missed spare or using poor form attempting to make the split, my corresponding sympathy was relatively low.

Every time he grimaced while lifting anything or it appeared like he was suffering, I made sure I acknowledged it with some sort of snide comment and general mockery.

When a couple of months passed with no improvement, he broke down and went to the doctor.

Though I wasn't there, I like to imagine how the visit went.

I can only assume they talked in bowling lingo, using terms like, 'approach,' and 'follow through' when discussing his arm and instead of notes, the doctor probably just wrote a bunch of "X's" and shaded triangles for reference in his medical chart.

Regardless, he came home with a tennis (bowling) elbow diagnosis and orders to wear a sort of weird, black band.

Doubtful that a two-inch strip of polyester, wrapped around his arm, was anything more than a sympathy ploy - let alone a cure for whatever he'd done - I went to work.

"Are you in mourning," I would ask when he wore it, "or is that what everyone's wearing at the office these days?"

It took some effort, but eventually my band shaming paid off. He stopped wearing it, and there was no further discussion of the bowling injury after that.

He must have recovered, even though his professional bowling career was clearly over, and I forgot all about it.

At least until one day last spring, when during a fierce, sweaty, Nike-commercial game of backyard badminton, I felt something go painfully awry in my arm.

Since it was still my serve, I obviously continued playing, but after a couple more flicks, it was apparent that something was seriously wrong.

Embarrassed to admit that I'd somehow suffered a catastrophic arm injury while volleying a large pencil eraser over a net, I mumbled, "I think I pulled a muscle," and quit.

For days I was in agony. From my elbow to my fingers, pain.

Through it, however, I came to understand the meaning of real hardship. I struggled to depress the spout of my hair mousse, I had to carry my purse on the other arm, and texting took a whole lot longer than usual.

Even so, I refused to go to the doctor. What would I say?

That I did it when I was going in for the spike? That it happened while executing a less-than-perfect birdie return?

It's been nearly a year. I'm not any better. And I still haven't gone to the doctor.

I'm pretty sure I know what he'll say. He'll diagnose me with badminton elbow and send me home with a black, polyester band, which given my history, I cannot wear, at least not while my husband's home.

In the meantime, I'm trying to make the best of it. There's always Advil and I've switched over to hair gel. I also put our badminton set behind some boxes in the basement. With any luck, no one will ever find it.

Made in the USA
Las Vegas, NV
04 April 2021